You Can Take Charge!

Level C

A Study Skills Curriculum

Zaner-Bloser

Reviewers:
Elizabeth Coates, Moss Side Middle School, Monroeville, Pennsylvania
Matthew A. Guyette, Lynnfield Middle School, Lynnfield, Massachusetts

Editorial Development: Kent Publishing Services

Design and Production: Signature Design Group

Photography:
Cover Photos: *(top)* Globus, Holway & Lobel, The Stock Market; *(all others)* George C. Anderson
page 4, Patrick Ramsey, International Stock; *page 8 (top)* Scott Barrow, International Stock; *(bottom)* Nova Development Corporation; *page 11,* Richard Pharaoh, International Stock; *page 16,* Tony Demin, International Stock; *page 18,* Scott Barrow, International Stock; *page 20,* Patrick Ramsey, International Stock; *page 22,* Patrick Ramsey, International Stock; *page 23,* Jay Thomas, International Stock; *page 24,* Laurie Bayer, International Stock; *page 26,* Bob Jacobson, International Stock; *page 28,* Arthur Tilley, FPG International; *page 30,* Scott Barrow, International Stock; *page 31,* Patrick Ramsey, International Stock; *page 33 (left)* Scott Barrow, International Stock; *(right)* Patrick Ramsey, International Stock; *page 34,* Arthur Tilley, FPG International; *page 36,* Radomir Samardzic, International Stock; *page 38,* Harold Lloyd, FPG International; *page 40,* Patrick Ramsey, International Stock; *page 42,* Hal Kern, International Stock; *page 44,* FPG International; *page 48,* George C. Anderson; *page 50,* Rob Gage, FPG International; *page 52,* George C. Anderson; *page 54,* Michael Krasowitz, FPG International; *page 56,* HWR Productions; *page 60,* Phyllis Picardi, International Stock; *page 64,* Corel Photo Library; *page 66,* George C. Anderson; *page 67,* George C. Anderson; *page 68,* Adobe Image Library; *page 70,* Patrick Ramsey, International Stock; *page 71,* Adobe Image Library; *page 72,* George C. Anderson; *page 78,* Corel Photo Library; *page 80,* Adobe Image Library; *page 84,* Adobe Image Library; *page 85,* Nova Development Corporation; *page 88,* Terry Qing, FPG International; *page 91,* Scott Barrow, International Stock; *page 93,* Adobe Image Library; *page 98,* Elliott Smith, International Stock; *page 99,* Artville LCC; *page 100,* Adobe Image Library; *page 104,* Richard Gaul, FPG International; *page 105,* Lindy Powers, International Stock

Illustrations: *page 47,* Stewart McKissick; *(all others)* Kevin Brown, Top Dog Studios

ISBN 0-7367-0001-3

Zaner-Bloser, Inc., P.O. Box 16764, Columbus, Ohio 43216-6764 (1-800-421-3018)

Printed in the United States of America

01 02 TPO 5 4 3

Table of Contents

Organizing Your Study Space

A Space of Your Own

You need to study. Getting a good education is your key to a bright future, and studying is an important part of your learning process.

The further along you go in school, the more studying you'll need to do. You need a good place to study. Your space doesn't have to be big or fancy. And it doesn't have to be like anyone else's study space. You might study best in your bedroom while a classmate prefers the kitchen. Or you may just use a corner of a room. You might even find that the library is the best place for you to study.

Your study space should be a place where you feel comfortable, a place where you can concentrate. Your study space needs to be a place where you can learn.

Where Do You Stand?

How does your study space measure up? Use the quiz below to find out. Read each statement and fill in the circle to rate your study space.

1. I study in a place that is free of distractions such as a television or people talking.

| Hardly Ever | ① | ② | ③ | ④ | ⑤ | Almost Always |

2. I use an uncluttered desk or table where I can spread out books and papers.

| Hardly Ever | ① | ② | ③ | ④ | ⑤ | Almost Always |

3. I have a box, drawer, or cabinet where I can keep notes, papers, reports, and tests.

| Hardly Ever | ① | ② | ③ | ④ | ⑤ | Almost Always |

4. I keep a supply of paper, pens, pencils, and other materials in a place where I can always find them.

| Hardly Ever | ① | ② | ③ | ④ | ⑤ | Almost Always |

5. I study near a lamp or other good light source.

| Hardly Ever | ① | ② | ③ | ④ | ⑤ | Almost Always |

6. I sit in a sturdy, comfortable chair when I study.

| Hardly Ever | ① | ② | ③ | ④ | ⑤ | Almost Always |

7. I feel comfortable and ready to concentrate in the space where I study.

| Hardly Ever | ① | ② | ③ | ④ | ⑤ | Almost Always |

Rate Yourself

To rate your study space, add up the numbers in the circles you filled in. Write your total in the box.

◆ If you scored over 28, congratulations! Your study space should give you a head start on your assignments.

◆ If you scored between 15 and 27, you're getting there. With a little extra planning, your study space will be just right.

◆ If you scored between 7 and 14, you definitely can improve your study habits. Finding the right place to study will help.

Be a Designer

In the space below, draw a floor plan for your ideal study space. Get serious. Don't let money be a consideration. Include any equipment and furniture you'd like. Make it your own perfect spot for reading, writing, thinking, and learning new things.

Spruce Up Your Study Space

In a small group, share the study spaces you just designed. Identify and discuss the features that you feel are most important. In the space below, list each feature and write a sentence to explain why you think it is important.

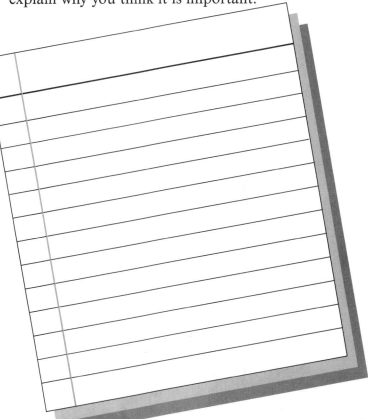

Now be creative. Choose one of the features you identified and write down how you could incorporate it into your study space. Try to think of ways to do it without spending any money. Maybe you can even recycle things you or your family already have.

The Right Space for You

Knickknacks or Not?

A good study environment for you may be different from a good study space for your best friend. Some students want to have an uncluttered study space, with no special mementos or favorite objects. They find these items distracting.

Other students want a more cozy, personal study space. They like to be surrounded by favorite things, such as family photographs on a bulletin board, a poster, or an old stuffed animal they've had since they were a baby.

Which picture appeals to you? Which study space seems more comfortable to you? In which space could you concentrate, study, and learn?

Organizing Your Materials

Have you ever sat down to write a report and realized that you left all your paper at school? Or have you ever spent an hour looking for a handout the teacher gave you the week before? When your study materials aren't well organized, you can lose valuable papers and time. Some materials should be with you all the time, whether you're at school or at home. Some should always be handy in your study space. And some, like computers or encyclopedias, may be things you use only at certain times. Even though you don't need to own these things, you should know how to find them quickly when you need them.

Make a list of materials you should keep in each place. If you're taking special classes like music, art, or advanced math, be sure to list the materials for those classes.

In my bookbag or backpack, I need:

_____

_____

_____

_____

In my study space, I need:

_____

_____

_____

_____

Special supplies I need to be able to find:

_____

_____

_____

_____

Make Your Study Space Grow

Can plants help you study better? Plants help remove pollutants from the air and increase the amount of oxygen in the environment. When the oxygen level in your study space rises, your productivity may increase, too.

Try it for yourself! Buy a few inexpensive plants in the discount store or ask permission to move some plants from another area of the house to your study space. See whether you feel more comfortable and productive with plants nearby. You might not notice an immediate change, but you can be sure that your area will be a healthier place to study.

Read It Right

Do you read with your books flat on a desk or tabletop? If so, how's your posture? Do you hunch over your book to read? Reading from a book that is lying flat isn't good for your posture. It may make your back or arms tired. It's not so good for your eyes, either. Most readers see more easily and become less tired when they prop up their books at a slight angle.

Try an experiment. The next time you have a long assignment to read, place your book at an angle. Use other books or a bookend to prop up your book. Find the angle that feels comfortable to you. See whether or not propping up your book helps your concentration.

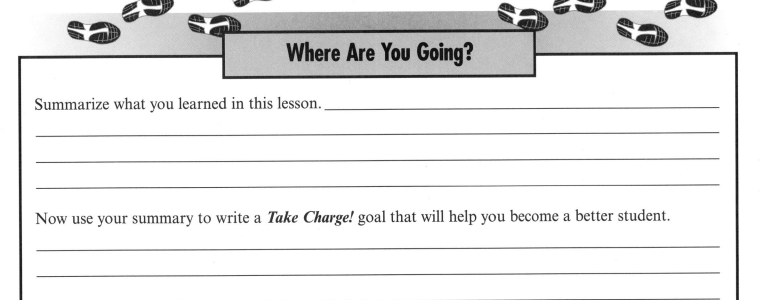

Where Are You Going?

Summarize what you learned in this lesson. _____

_____

_____

_____

Now use your summary to write a *Take Charge!* goal that will help you become a better student.

_____

_____

_____

Planning Work and Free Time

Anna does her homework right after school because she feels good when it is done. Then she can relax, talk on the phone, watch TV, or read a good book after dinner.

Steve has basketball practice after school. He starts his homework every night right after dinner—usually about 7:00 p.m.

Scheduling Strategies

Anna and Steve set schedules that allow them to get their homework done and also spend time doing things they enjoy. Sound impossible? It's not. Taking a little time to make a schedule will help you fit everything in!

Where Do You Stand?

What would you do if you had the time? Of course you have things like school, homework, chores, and family responsibilities to do every day. But there's more to life than chores! Make a check mark in front of one or two new activities you would like to fit into your schedule. Use the blank spaces to list any other activities you think you might like to try.

- [ ] join a club
- [ ] play a sport
- [ ] do community service work
- [ ] sing in a choir
- [ ] draw or paint
- [ ] write
- [ ] read for pleasure
- [ ] spend more time with family and friends
- [ ] explore a career
- [ ] _____
- [ ] _____
- [ ] _____
- [ ] _____

Make a Weekly Schedule

Going to school is a full-time job. In the after-school hours, you need to find time for homework, activities, chores, meals, sleep, relaxation, and a little fun, too. Can you fit it all in? Of course you can! You just need to plan your time well.

On the weekly planner pages below, record your schedule for next week. Decide on a firm block of time to study each day. Set a consistent time to go to bed. Then see if you can find a time slot to fit in one of the new activities you checked on page 8.

Week of _____

	Monday	Tuesday	Wednesday
7:00			
8:00			
9:00			
10:00			
11:00			
12:00			
1:00			
2:00			
3:00			
4:00			
5:00			
6:00			
7:00			
8:00			
9:00			
10:00			

Thursday	Friday	Saturday	
			8:00
			9:00
			10:00
			11:00
			12:00
			1:00
			2:00
			3:00
			4:00
			5:00
			6:00
			7:00
			8:00
			9:00
			10:00

		Sunday	
			8:00
			9:00
			10:00
			11:00
			12:00
			1:00
			2:00
			3:00
			4:00
			5:00
			6:00
			7:00
			8:00
			9:00
			10:00

Tips for Scheduling Your Time

Start a "To-Do" List

A weekly schedule is a good thing to have, but you may find that it's too general to keep you on track every day. To make sure you're completing all the tasks you need to accomplish each day, you may want to make a daily to-do list.

Your daily to-do list includes all the tasks you need to do each day to keep yourself on schedule. It may include homework assignments, chores, after-school activities, and plans with friends. Check your to-do list every morning. Each night before you go to bed, check your to-do list again. Cross off every task you've completed. Then make a new to-do list for the next day. Put any tasks you didn't complete on tomorrow's list.

TO DO

Feed the cat
Study for test
Go to practice
Do math homework
Take out the trash
Read next chapter for English
Call for concert tickets

If you find that you hardly ever accomplish everything on your list, you may be underestimating the time you need for each task. Take a hard look at your schedule. Are you forgetting to schedule travel time or time for snacks and breaks? Do you need to allow more time for your homework? You may need to revise your schedule.

Prioritize Your List

You have many different jobs to do every day. Some are more important than others. Some tasks, like studying for tests, lead to important life goals. Others, like feeding your fish, are so easy to do that they seem trivial, but they are important, too. Some need to be done, but they don't need to be completed right away. Other jobs on your list really don't matter very much at all. It won't hurt to put them off until tomorrow. In fact, it may not matter if you never get around to them at all.

The problem is that those less important activities are often easier and more enjoyable than the important ones. It's tempting to do the easy job instead of the harder but more important one. What would you rather do—start a big science project or arrange your CD collection?

Sometimes it's hard to make the right choice. Just remember, you need to make sure the important things get done. Take a good hard look at your list and prioritize your work. Decide which tasks are important. Then make sure you get them done.

To prioritize your to-do list, decide which of your obligations are most urgent. Write a number *1* in front of these jobs. Then decide which things are least urgent. Give these a number *3*. Finally, place a number *2* next to the other tasks that come between—the things that have to get done but not right now. Then work through the jobs on your list, starting with the most urgent. Cross off each job as you complete it.

Scheduling Tips

- **Set realistic goals.** Giving yourself two hours to complete a four-hour job just sets you up for failure.

- **Avoid marathon study sessions.** Working on science for an hour a day for a week is usually easier and more productive than doing six hours of science on Sunday evening. When you schedule a study marathon for yourself, you're likely to find that it's hard to stay focused and efficient.

- **Allow time for chores and errands.** Don't forget to schedule everyday tasks such as doing dishes or walking your dog.

- **Schedule time for fun.** It's important to have fun. After you've let yourself "waste" a little time, you'll find that it's easier to settle down to work.

- **Plan a regular time for study.** When you study at the same time every day, studying will become part of your daily routine. You'll find it easier to get started and to stay focused.

- **Stick to your schedule.** Once you've started to work, don't let any distractions interrupt your study time.

- **Reward yourself.** Schedule a reward, like playing a video game, watching television, or calling a friend, after each difficult task. Your reward will give you an incentive to keep going.

- **Take time to plan.** Schedule ten minutes each evening to plan your time for the next day. When morning comes, you'll be all ready to go.

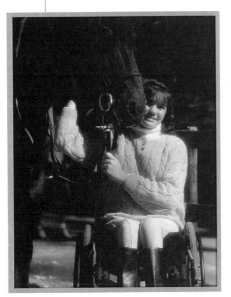

School is a full-time job. But you can get your schoolwork done and still have time left over to do things you enjoy by trying some of these tips.

Where Are You Going?

Summarize what you learned in this lesson. _____

_____

_____

_____

Now use your summary to write a *Take Charge!* goal that will help you become a better student.

_____

_____

_____

Setting Goals

A journey of 1,000 miles begins with one step.

—Chinese Proverb

GETTING THERE

When you set off on a trip, you usually know where you're going. You know where your journey begins, and a map shows just how to get to your destination. Working to accomplish a life goal is a different kind of journey. Unfortunately, the path to accomplishing a life goal like going to college or having a career isn't always clear. You need to set a goal and stick to it, no matter what. One thing's for sure. You'll never get there until you take that first step. And that first step is setting your goal.

Where Do You Stand?

How good are you at setting goals? Check each statement that is usually true for you.

☐ I regularly plan and schedule my time.

☐ I make daily to-do lists.

☐ I seldom feel behind in my work.

☐ I finish projects in a timely fashion.

☐ I rarely have to give excuses for not getting things done.

☐ I have clear, specific daily goals I want to accomplish.

☐ I have short-term goals for things I want to accomplish this year.

☐ I have long-term goals for becoming the person I want to be, and I make choices to help me achieve them.

Rate Yourself

◆ If you checked all eight statements, congratulations! You have excellent goal-setting habits.

◆ If you checked between three and seven of the statements, you can use some practice with setting realistic goals.

◆ If you checked only one or two statements, you'll find that setting goals will help you make the most of your time.

Long-Term Goals

Long-term goals are goals you set now and achieve in the future. Long-term goals may take five, fifteen, or even twenty-five years to achieve. To set a long-term goal, imagine what you want your life to be like in the future. Where will you be? Who will you become?

Brainstorm a list of your long-term goals and write them on the lines. Don't worry, long-term plans aren't set in stone; they will change as you learn more about yourself and the world.

_____

_____

_____

_____

_____

_____

Talk About It

Now get together with a small group of classmates. Pretend that you're attending a middle school reunion twenty years from now. Imagine that you're sitting around a dinner table. Tell what you've accomplished in the years since you last saw each other.

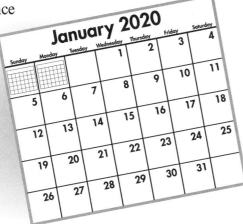

Short-Term Goals

Short-term goals are goals you can accomplish in a few months or a year. Brainstorm a list of things you would like to accomplish before the beginning of the next school year. Include steps that lead toward your long-term goals, as well as activities you find satisfying and enjoyable.

_____

_____

_____

_____

Daily Goals

Daily goals tell you exactly what you can do today to move your life ahead in the right direction. Most daily goals are small steps toward short-term goals. Lists of daily goals are also called to-do lists. Remember, as you complete things on your to-do list, cross them off. At the end of each day, make a new to-do list for the next day.

Make a to-do list for tomorrow on the lines below.

_____

_____

_____

_____

_____

_____

Chart Your Course (Near and Far)

Tips for Goal-Setting

◆ Make your goals clear, specific, and measurable. For example, *I will complete and turn in every homework assignment in social studies* is clearer than *I will do better in social studies.*

◆ Be sure your goals are realistic and achievable. Set goals that are within your reach.

◆ Phrase your goals positively. For example, *I will pass all my math quizzes* is much more encouraging than *I'm not going to get any Fs.*

◆ Set a reasonable number of goals. If you make too many goals, you may be so confused you won't accomplish any of them.

◆ Think of achieving your goals as a game and a challenge rather than a chore.

◆ Team up with a friend. Cheer for each other whenever one of you accomplishes a goal. Encourage each other when reaching a goal seems too hard.

◆ Be patient. Don't expect to meet your goals immediately. It takes time to learn new habits.

◆ Have confidence in yourself. Having a positive attitude will help you reach your goals.

◆ Don't be afraid to adjust your goals. Everyone changes as they grow. Sometimes goals change, too.

Motivate Yourself

Whenever you sit down to set goals, keep in mind your reasons for making them. Goals can keep you focused. If you understand that it's necessary to study math now to get into college later, you'll feel better about finishing those math problems each night. Goals are your motivation, or driving force, for being in school, studying, and learning.

Reach for the Stars

When you were a young child, you may have planned to be a professional athlete or a movie star. By now you probably realize that very few people reach those peaks. Some careers require special talents that people are born with. Be realistic, but don't let your realistic attitude keep you from aiming high. And don't be afraid to try hard things or things that take a long time. If you set goals that are too easy to reach, you may be disappointed later.

Keep Track of Your Goals

Write your long- and short-term goals on note cards. Post your goals in places where you will see them often, such as in your school locker, on your bulletin board, or on your bathroom mirror. Your written goals will be constant and motivating reminders of what you're trying to achieve.

My Goals

Sample Long-Term Goals:

- Buy a car
- Travel to another country
- Own a company
- Become a pilot
- Graduate from college
- Get married and raise a family
- Help solve problems in the world
- Become an expert in a field that interests me

Sample Short-Term Goals:

- Raise my math grade by one letter
- Act in the school play
- Learn to throw a curve ball
- Save money to buy a CD player
- Become a starter on the team
- Read three books a month
- Build a model airplane
- Work out three times a week

Sample Daily Goals:

- Complete math homework
- Baby-sit for my neighbor
- Practice pitching for one-half hour
- Do the dishes
- Mow the lawn
- Take out the trash
- Make an appointment with my guidance counselor
- Set up a sleepover for the weekend

Where Are You Going?

Summarize what you learned in this lesson. _____

_____

_____

_____

Now use your summary to write a *Take Charge!* goal that will help you become a better student.

_____

_____

_____

LESSON 4

Developing Healthy Habits

A healthy body leads to a healthy mind.

To Your Health

Do you think schoolwork takes up so much time that you don't have time to practice healthy habits? Think again. When your body runs down, so does your brain power. You get tired more easily, and you find it harder to concentrate.

Make habits like exercising, getting enough sleep, and eating a healthy diet a part of your daily schedule. You may find that you have so much extra energy that you have more time, not less!

Where Do You Stand?

Take inventory of your health habits. Think carefully. Then write honest answers to the questions below.

1. How many hours of sleep do you usually get on school nights? _____

2. How many glasses of water do you usually drink every day? _____

3. List the snack foods you eat most often. Then put a star beside the ones you think are healthy for you.

_____

_____

_____

4. Make a list of the kinds of exercise you do every week. Remember to list activities like walking to school or taking gym class.

_____

_____

_____

5. Think about the last meal you ate. Rate it on a scale of 1 to 5.

Very Healthy	①	②	③	④	⑤	Junk Food

Rate Yourself

Did the quiz make you think? Just how good are your health habits? Our bodies are all different. They may have slightly different requirements. But a good rule of thumb is to get about eight hours of sleep a night, drink eight glasses of water a day, eat mostly grains, fruits, and vegetables, and work at least half an hour of exercise into your daily schedule.

Take a Sleep Survey

Sleep deprivation is common among teenagers. It often accounts for low grades, poor health, and bad dispositions. Getting a good night's sleep should be one of your daily goals.

In a small group, design a survey to find out the average number of hours students in your school sleep at night. Compare two groups of students like boys and girls in your class or students in different grades. Plan your survey on the lines below.

The two groups of students we'll study are:

_____

_____

Our survey questions will be:

_____

_____

_____

_____

After your group completes the poll, tally the results. Add the total number of sleep hours for the first group and divide by the number of people interviewed for that group. This will give you the average. Repeat for the second group. Report your results to the class.

Plan for Healthy Eating

Study the food guide pyramid. If you're like many people, you probably eat more foods from the top of the pyramid than is healthy for you.

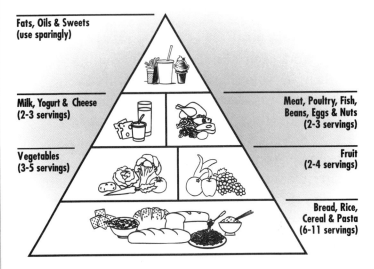

Fats, Oils & Sweets (use sparingly)

Milk, Yogurt & Cheese (2-3 servings)

Meat, Poultry, Fish, Beans, Eggs & Nuts (2-3 servings)

Vegetables (3-5 servings)

Fruit (2-4 servings)

Bread, Rice, Cereal & Pasta (6-11 servings)

You can improve your eating habits by planning ahead. List your favorite foods from each group.

◆ **Bread, Rice, Cereal, and Pasta** _____

_____

◆ **Vegetables** _____

_____

◆ **Fruit** _____

_____

◆ **Milk, Yogurt, and Cheese** _____

_____

◆ **Meat, Poultry, Fish, Beans, Eggs, and Nuts**

_____

_____

◆ **Fats, Oils, and Sweets** _____

_____

You Can Make Healthy Choices

Exercise, Exercise, Exercise!

Work exercise into your daily routine whenever you can. Regular physical exercise keeps your muscles and heart in good shape. It can also reduce stress, tension, and anxiety. It may not be as hard as you think to find ways to exercise. You can do stretches even while you're sitting down. And sometimes you can walk or ride your bike instead of asking for a ride in the car. Even cleaning up your room is good exercise!

The Eyes Have It

Eyestrain can give you a headache. It also makes it hard for you to concentrate. Always read and work under a good light. Natural light and incandescent lighting are better for your eyes than fluorescent lighting. If you get headaches or have trouble concentrating when you read, ask for an eye test.

Healthy Snacks

Remember the food guide pyramid? It can help you plan healthy snacks. We should all eat three to five servings of vegetables a day and two to four servings of fruit. Remember that it's just as easy to snack on a carrot or some fruit as it is to grab a candy bar. It's better for you, too!

Take Care of Those Teeth

Brush your teeth at least twice a day. If possible, carry a toothbrush so you can brush after every meal. Healthy teeth and gums are important for many reasons. Did you know that infected teeth and gums can cause serious health problems? An infection that starts in your mouth can travel to other parts of your body.

Turn a Frown Upside Down

Keep smiling! Smiling is much easier than frowning. Did you know that it takes only about seventeen muscles to smile? When you frown, you use forty-three muscles.

A positive attitude is very healthy.

Water, Water Everywhere

Drink eight glasses of water a day to keep your body working at its best. Soft drinks and fruit juices don't count. You really need to drink plain old water!

Eat Like an Athlete

Research shows that athletes who eat starchy, carbohydrate-rich diets have better endurance than athletes on high protein diets.

The ideal diet for an athlete includes potatoes, whole grain noodles, rice, bread, beans, peas, raw or steamed vegetables, and small amounts of meat, eggs, and milk. This diet is low in butter, sugar, and other fattening foods.

If you get lots of exercise, an athlete's diet might give you more energy. Try adding more carbohydrates to your diet for a short period of time. See if you have extra energy.

Carbohydrates are a main source of fuel for the muscles and the brain.

You Are *When* You Eat

Even if you eat a healthy diet, you may find yourself feeling tired, grouchy, or unable to concentrate at certain times of the day. Your diet can cause these feelings. Too much sugar at one time may cause you to feel very energetic for a while. But when the sugar wears off, you may feel extremely tired, or even sad and depressed. A big meal may taste good, but you may feel sleepy afterward. Sometimes you may not even realize that you're hungry. If you find you can't concentrate, a healthy snack may help.

To see how eating affects your moods, try keeping a food/mood log. Write down everything you eat and the time you eat it. Whenever your mood changes, write it in the log. See if you can find a pattern or a connection between your food intake and your moods. Even if you can't control the times when you eat, you'll often be able to control what you eat and how much you eat.

Where Are You Going?

Summarize what you learned in this lesson. _____

_____

_____

_____

Now use your summary to write a ***Take Charge!*** goal that will help you become a better student.

_____

_____

_____

Managing Distractions

STAY TUNED FOR . . .

R-r-ring! R-r-ring!
Leesa, telephone!

Arf! Arf! Arf!

Distractions Are Everywhere!

You're all set to study. You've got your books and materials together. You've enjoyed a snack. You've changed into comfortable clothes. You've planned your whole evening, and you're even looking forward to getting your math homework out of the way and completing a long social studies project.

But things don't go quite the way you planned. The doorbell rings, and then your cousin who lives out of town calls. The cat sits on your papers, and the dog won't stop barking until you play fetch. When you finally get to work, you can't keep yourself from listening to the TV show that's on in the next room.

Does this sound familiar? Everyone's life is full of distractions. You just need to learn how to deal with them.

Where Do You Stand?

What would you do in these situations? Circle the approach you think would work best for you.

Situation 1:
It's late afternoon. You're doing your homework. A friend calls and wants to get together. What do you do?

a. Finish your homework quickly so you can meet your friend later.

b. Meet your friend and do your homework later.

c. Tell your friend that you need to study, but you'd like to get together another day.

d. Tell your friend you can't get together, then chat on the phone for an hour.

Situation 2:
You have a big test tomorrow, and there's a great movie on television. What do you do?

a. Review your notes during commercials.

b. Watch the movie and then stay up as late as you can to study for your test.

c. Rent the movie from the video store and watch it another night.

d. Do your studying quickly so you have time to watch the second half of the movie.

Rate Yourself

If you chose answer *c* for both questions, you know how to stick to a task. If you chose any other answers, you sometimes let distractions get in the way of doing your best work. Read on to learn how to get control of the distractions in your life.

Distractions, Distractions

What is distracting for one person may be soothing background noise for another person. For most people, though, the fewer distractions you have, the better you concentrate and the more efficiently you work.

In a small group, brainstorm a list of things that can be distracting when you're trying to study. Consider physical distractions in your environment that you can see, hear, touch, taste, or smell, and mental distractions inside your own head. Write your ideas below. Then reread your list and star the distractions that are most annoying to you.

Take Control

Make a list of at least five specific steps you could take to reduce distractions in your study environment. For example, your list might include making a rule for yourself, such as *No TV while studying!* or hanging a *Do Not Disturb* sign on the bedroom door.

_____

_____

_____

_____

_____

_____

_____

Put the ideas on your list into practice for the next two weeks. Keep track of your school performance during this time. If your schoolwork improves, you'll know that your study environment has been affecting your school performance. It would be smart to incorporate these distraction reducers into your regular study routine.

Tips for Dealing With Distractions

Quiet, Please!

Studying in a quiet place might improve your grades. Comprehension rates usually decrease in direct proportion to the amount of sound in your environment. Try this experiment to find out how noise affects you.

Find a short poem. Memorize the first half of the poem with loud music or noise in the background. Spend as much time as you need to be able to write the lines perfectly from memory. Make a note of how much time you spent. Then turn off the music and find a quiet place to memorize the other half of the poem. Again, time yourself. Compare the amounts of time you spent memorizing each half of the poem. Did distracting noises affect your concentration?

Make Use of "White" Noise

If you find that noise affects you, you can sometimes turn off the sound and work in a quiet place. But some noises, like street or family sounds, cannot be turned off. In that case, you might be able to cover the sounds with "white" noise. White noise is bland, repetitive noise like the hum of a fan or rain falling on the roof. Your mind soon gets used to the sound of white noise and tunes it out. Since you're close to the source of the noise, it can hide louder sounds that are farther away.

Get Rid of Inner Distractions

In addition to physical distractions in your environment, "inner noise" can also interrupt your concentration. Inner noise is made up of thoughts, worries, and daydreams that keep running through your mind. It can be every bit as disturbing as noise from outside sources. It's hard to turn off your inner noise, but you need to do it if you're going to be able to concentrate. Tell yourself to focus on one thing at a time. Promise yourself that you'll think, worry, and daydream later.

Try this technique for clearing your mind. When you sit down to study, take a moment to calm yourself. Keep a blank sheet of paper handy. Write down thoughts that are taking up your attention. Get them out of your head and onto the paper. Whenever new distracting thoughts intrude, add them to your list. You can deal with them when you've finished your studying.

Music Can Make You Smarter

Some kinds of music have the same effect as white noise. Try tuning your radio to an "easy listening" station that plays soft music without sudden loud tones or distracting lyrics. Or listen to classical music. Studies have shown that certain pieces of classical music help your mind focus. Classical music can even make you work "smarter."

Try listening to classical music when you study. You might find it helps you concentrate.

Find the Best Place to Study

Some places have built-in distractions. You can't always expect everything to stop just because you want to study. Your family may not be willing to turn off the television just because you plan to study for a test in the living room. And if you have brothers or sisters, they probably won't be quiet on command! You may need to change your own study schedule to cut out distractions.

If your usual study space has too many distractions, be creative. Can you study in the library after school or at an after-school homework center? Is there a corner of a bedroom you could turn into your own special study spot at certain times? Some people even use a closet for their own private "office."

Talk Over the Problem

Don't be afraid to discuss the problem of distractions with friends, family members, or your school counselor. Let your friends know when your scheduled study times are. Ask them to call at a different time or to be understanding when you say you will call them back later. Your family members may be able to come up with ideas you haven't even thought of for providing a quiet time or a new place for you to study. And a counselor or teacher may be willing to let you study in an empty classroom or may know of an after-school program you weren't aware of. Once you make up your mind to be more focused on your studies, you may be surprised how much others are willing to help.

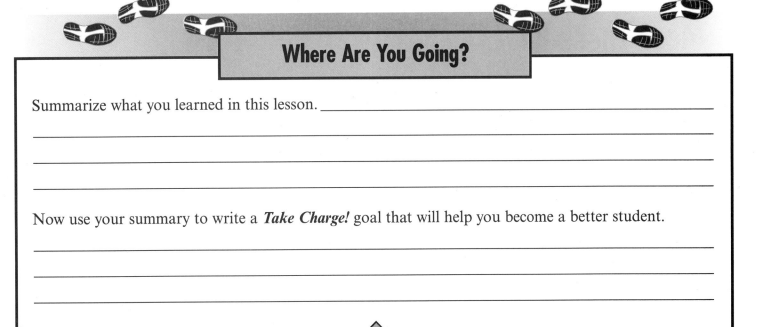

Where Are You Going?

Summarize what you learned in this lesson. _____
_____
_____
_____

Now use your summary to write a *Take Charge!* goal that will help you become a better student.
_____
_____
_____
_____

Identifying Strengths and Weaknesses

Tina likes to peer tutor younger students. Rachel is head of the school's can food drive. Jackie is captain of the field hockey team.

Meet These Best Friends

Tina, Rachel, and Jackie are best friends, yet they are involved in very different activities. Tina has strong academic skills. She has an ability to learn new things quickly. That's why she volunteers to help other students. Rachel is an organizer. She can manage multiple tasks and coordinate large projects. Jackie is good at motivating people. She has the ability to work well with her teammates.

All three girls are capitalizing on their strengths. Everyone has different strengths and weaknesses. What are yours?

Where Do You Stand?

Just like Tina, Rachel, and Jackie, all people are stronger in some situations and weaker in others. Read the situations below. Circle *Strong* or *Weak* to show how you'd feel about handling each situation.

1. It's time to take a big test in your favorite subject.

   Strong   Weak

2. Your best friend's dog died, and he feels very sad.

   Strong   Weak

3. Your little sister got into your room and pulled everything off the shelves. What a mess! How will you ever get everything back together?

   Strong   Weak

4. Your teacher has asked you to tutor a new student.

   Strong   Weak

5. Your two best friends are having an argument. They say they'll never speak again.

   Strong   Weak

6. Your club is organizing a charity food drive and you've been asked to lead the project.

   Strong   Weak

Rate Yourself

There are many different kinds of skills and talents. You may be strong in academics, music, art, organizational skills, or in working with people. The quiz assesses your skills in three areas: academics, people skills, and organization. If you circled *Strong* for questions 1 and 4, you feel that academics is a strength. If you circled *Strong* for questions 2 and 5, people skills may be your strength. If you circled *Strong* for 3 and 6, your organizational skills are probably strong.

Role Models

Everyone has strengths and weaknesses. That doesn't mean that one person is better than another. It simply means that people learn and perform activities in a variety of ways based on their strengths.

In a small group, brainstorm a list of people that you know who are particularly strong in the areas listed below. These people can be class-mates, family members, or famous people. After you have listed several people in each category, discuss what skills they possess that make them good at what they do.

People with strong organizational skills

_____

_____

People with strong academic skills

_____

_____

People with strong skills in working with other people

_____

_____

Take Inventory

Take inventory of your own strengths and weaknesses. For each category below, list activities that you feel you have accomplished successfully. Don't worry if you don't have a long list in every category.

Organizational tasks

Academic tasks

Tasks working with other people

Are you better at some types of tasks than others? Once you understand what comes naturally to you, you can develop strategies to help you capitalize on your strengths and minimize your weaknesses.

Capitalize on Your Strengths

Different Kinds of Strengths

People have many different kinds of strengths. They may have special talents in music and art, academics, athletics, working with people, or organizing. You may have strengths in more than one area and weaknesses in more than one area.

Since you've been a student most of your life, the emphasis has probably been on your academic strengths. Your ability to learn is an important skill you will use all your life. But as you leave school to go to work, you'll find that employers also value teamwork, or people skills. Teamwork skills include being a leader, doing your part to carry out your group's goals, and getting along with others.

Employers also value personal management and organizational skills. These skills range from the ability to get to work on time to a talent for setting up a plan for accomplishing goals within a time frame.

Learning Strengths

Your strengths are reflected in the ways you learn. Some people learn best by listening. Some learn best by seeing. And some learn best by touching or moving things around. How do you learn best?

Auditory Mode: People who learn best by listening are *auditory learners*. You may be an auditory learner if you remember the tunes and lyrics of songs easily. Auditory learners generally find it easy to remember what their teachers say in class.

Visual Mode: People who learn best by seeing are *visual learners*. If you easily remember what you read, you may be a visual learner. Can you close your eyes and picture the details of something you've only seen a few times? Then you may be a visual learner, too. Most painters and photographers are visual learners.

Tactile or Kinesthetic Mode: People who learn best by touching or doing are *tactile* or *kinesthetic learners*. Do you have to write down a telephone number before you can remember it? Then your learning strength may be tactile. If you like to work on crafts or perform science experiments, you're probably a kinesthetic learner. Dancers who remember complicated sequences of steps are often kinesthetic learners.

Make it your goal to develop strengths in these three areas: ability to learn, teamwork, and personal management and organization.

Compensating for Weaknesses

There are two ways to approach weaknesses. One is to work hard to turn your weakness into a strength. If you have trouble organizing, improve this skill by making lists and schedules.

The other is to try to compensate for a weakness by using a strength. If you're a tactile learner in a lecture class, turn what you hear into good written notes. The act of writing will burn the ideas into your brain. If you are a visual learner, take notes in the form of webs or pictures whenever possible.

Working to Your Strengths

Once you become aware of your strengths, find ways to use them whenever you can. If people skills are your strength, organize a study group before the next test. If you're an auditory learner, make an audiotape of your social studies notes to learn them.

The most important thing is to learn to like the person you are and the strengths you have. The next time you face a challenge, like a big test or a major project, you'll feel ready to use your strengths to tackle it head on!

Assess Yourself

Think about what you've learned about strengths. Then write a brief answer for each of the following questions.

1. Is your ability to learn one of your strengths? How could you improve your learning skills?

_____

_____

2. Do you like to work on teams? How could you improve your teamwork skills?

_____

_____

3. Are you well organized? Do you manage time well? How could you improve your personal management and organizational skills?

_____

_____

4. What is your strongest learning mode: auditory, visual, or tactile/kinesthetic? Why do you think you learn best in this mode?

_____

_____

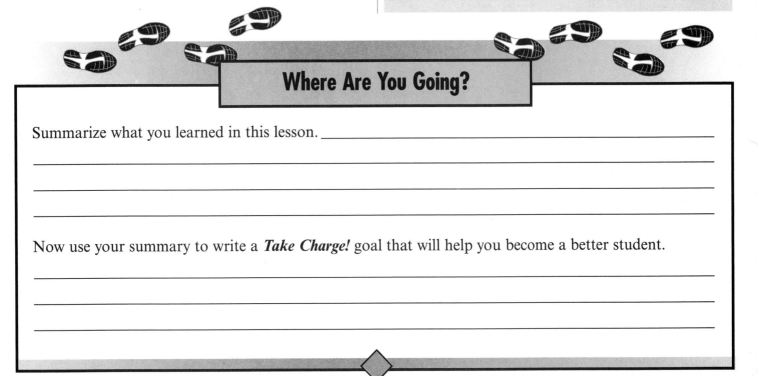

Where Are You Going?

Summarize what you learned in this lesson. _____

_____

_____

_____

Now use your summary to write a *Take Charge!* goal that will help you become a better student.

_____

_____

_____

Resisting Negative Influences

Who Are Your Friends?

Now that you're older, you're responsible for making some decisions on your own. But it's a big world out there! It's tough to make decisions all by yourself. You need good friends around to support you.

You've probably noticed, though, that some of your old friends are changing. Some may even be trying out things you think are wrong or dangerous. And they may want you to try those things along with them. Negative peer pressure can get in the way of good judgment. It's important to choose friends who want the best for you.

Where Do You Stand?

How good are you at resisting negative peer pressure? Take the quiz below to find out. Read each statement and mark the scale to show how often you respond this way.

1. You have a Spanish test last period. At lunch, you take a copy of the test offered from a friend who took the test in the first period.

| Hardly Ever | ① | ② | ③ | ④ | ⑤ | Almost Always |

2. You know you have to practice for your recital. A friend asks you to go to the movies so you do that instead.

| Hardly Ever | ① | ② | ③ | ④ | ⑤ | Almost Always |

3. You don't raise your hand to answer questions in class anymore because your friends laughed at your answer the last time.

| Hardly Ever | ① | ② | ③ | ④ | ⑤ | Almost Always |

4. You have a brother who did the same science project last year and offered to give it to you. You copy it and turn it in as your own.

| Hardly Ever | ① | ② | ③ | ④ | ⑤ | Almost Always |

5. You have a big test tomorrow. But there is a television show on late tonight that all your friends will be watching. You need a good night's sleep for the test but you watch the show anyway.

| Hardly Ever | ① | ② | ③ | ④ | ⑤ | Almost Always |

Rate Yourself

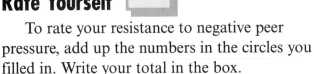

To rate your resistance to negative peer pressure, add up the numbers in the circles you filled in. Write your total in the box.

◆ If you scored under 8, congratulations! You are taking control of your own actions. Read on for more helpful tips.

◆ If you scored between 8 and 16, you might be letting your friends influence you a little too much. You can improve your decisions by trying some of the strategies in this lesson.

◆ If you scored over 16, you may need to rethink how you choose and interact with your friends.

Stand Up for Yourself

It's natural to be curious about new activities, but most people understand that some things are just plain wrong. What things are wrong? Well, things that are unhealthy or illegal are wrong. And sometimes the things that get in the way of reaching your goals are wrong.

Often it's enough just to avoid people who have different values. But once in a while you're likely to find yourself alone in a group of people who think differently than you. When that happens, saying *no* can be hard. The key to saying *no* is planning ahead.

On the lines below, write your best strategies for avoiding going along with the crowd.

_____

_____

_____

_____

_____

_____

Saying *No*

Saying *no* is a skill. Like most skills, it takes practice. Form a small group with two other classmates. Make up three situations in which someone your age might need to say *no*. Describe the situations on the lines below.

Situation 1: _____

_____

_____

_____

_____

Situation 2: _____

_____

_____

_____

_____

Situation 3: _____

_____

_____

_____

_____

Now role-play the situations and demonstrate ways to say *no*. Take turns being the people who are pressuring and the person who is saying *no*. Use techniques you wrote about earlier or make up new ones as you go along. Choose your best skit and act it out for the class.

Tips for Managing Peer Pressure

Choose Your Friends Wisely

There's an old saying you've probably heard from your parents: *You are judged by the company you keep.* This means that if you hang around with people who act in a certain way, other people will think you believe the actions are okay. You need to choose your friends wisely. As you grow up, you'll keep some of your old friends, and you'll also make new ones. Remember that a friend is not just someone who lives nearby or someone you've always known. A friend is a person who cares about you. It's a person who doesn't always have to be the boss, a person who listens to what you say and accepts your feelings. If your friends won't take no for an answer, you probably have the wrong friends.

You are judged by the company you keep.

Can We Talk?

When you're having problems with peer pressure, don't be afraid to ask for advice. You can talk to friends your own age. You can also talk to family members, teachers, counselors, or people you know from community activities. Choose a person you trust, and choose your words carefully. Speak in general terms if you want to. That means you don't need to name names—you can say "a classmate" or "someone I know."

Choose Your Battles

Sometimes you can solve a problem just by avoiding the person who is pressuring you or by walking away. Sometimes you may want to take the time and trouble to explain your feelings or to try to talk your friend out of whatever he or she is planning.

What you decide to do may depend on the seriousness of the situation. If you think your friend is getting into real trouble, you may decide to try to convince your friend that the action is wrong. If you're not sure, you can ask a trusted adult to help you decide.

Keep Your Goals in Mind

There are different kinds of peer pressure. A friend may try to pressure you into doing something like going to a movie instead of doing your homework. Or, a friend may try to pressure you into doing something more serious like skipping school, smoking, or using alcohol and other drugs. Just keep your personal goals in mind and consider the consequences of your decisions. Make the decisions that lead you toward a healthy, happy, and productive future.

When choosing your friends, be sure to keep your personal goals in mind.

Ways to Say No

Just say it.
Start by saying a simple, "No, thank you." Don't anticipate an argument. Maybe no one will pressure you after all.

Walk away.
No one can pressure you if you're not there. If a situation looks like trouble, avoid it.

Suggest an alternative.
If you don't want to do what a friend suggests, present another option. If you need to do your homework, your friend probably does, too. Ask your friend to skip the movie and study with you instead.

Explain your reasons.
You never have to say anything except *no*. But sometimes you'll want to explain your reasons. A friend who is pressuring you to forget about your homework may not realize that your grades are especially important to you because you want to stay eligible for sports. Once you've explained the situation, you may never be pressured again.

Enlist help.
If the pressure doesn't stop, ask an adult for help. The adult can give you advice or intervene on your behalf.

Where Are You Going?

Summarize what you learned in this lesson. _____

_____

_____

_____

Now use your summary to write a *Take Charge!* goal that will help you become a better student.

_____

_____

_____

_____

LESSON 8

Solving Problems in a Group

Teamwork is fun when it works. But sometimes a team needs a little coaching.

Join the Team

Solving problems can be tricky. And working with a group to solve a problem or complete a project can be even trickier. Differences of opinion and uncooperative behavior can make the time some groups spend together frustrating and unproductive.

You probably already recognize the symptoms of "sick group syndrome." It happens when some group members dominate the conversation, some joke around or disrupt the group, and others just tune out. The good news is that there are strategies you can learn to help make group work more productive and a lot more fun.

You probably make more group decisions than you realize. A group can be anything from yourself and one other person to a whole classroom. In both cases, you need to work together.

Below is a list of places in which you spend part of your school day. For every location, describe a situation in which you need to solve a problem in a group.

1. Gym _____

_____

_____

2. Lunchroom _____

_____

_____

3. Classroom _____

_____

_____

4. School bus _____

_____

_____

5. Hallway _____

_____

_____

Rate Yourself

Think about the group problem-solving situations you described. Do you enjoy making decisions in a group or would you rather decide on your own? Take a poll to see how many students in your class enjoy group work and how many have had negative experiences with group work.

Work on Your Own

Whether or not you like group work, you will face many situations that require you to work with others. Everyone can learn and practice strategies to make group work go more smoothly. Use your own experiences with group work to give advice to the student below. Work by yourself to write your advice.

Four of us are in the middle of an important social studies project. We have to be ready to present it to the class next week. The project—and the grade—are really important to me. Unfortunately, there's this one guy in our group who keeps clowning around. I'd like to just tell him off—but when other members of the group do that, he actually seems to enjoy it. What do I do?

_____

_____

_____

_____

_____

Work With a Group

Now form a group with three or four classmates. Read the problem below and write some advice. This time, work together to find a solution everyone in the group agrees on.

A group of us are planning a dance. When we got together last week, I had as many ideas as anyone, but no one seemed willing to listen. If these weren't my friends, I'd probably just quit.

_____

_____

_____

_____

_____

_____

Compare the Processes

Which advice was easier to write—the advice you wrote alone or the advice you wrote in a group? Why?

_____

_____

_____

_____

Tips for Group Problem Solving

Six Basic Steps

1. State the problem.

Stating the problem may sound easy, but making a decision about the group's purpose can be a problem. Listen to everyone's ideas and list the alternatives on a chart. Agree on a problem statement to make sure your group's purpose is clear to everyone.

2. Brainstorm.

You want lots of serious ideas, so encourage everyone to speak out. Accept any idea at this point. Discussing or criticizing ideas can end the discussion quickly. Even an idea that obviously won't work can lead to another idea that will.

3. Choose one or more ideas to try out.

Vote on each idea. If an idea doesn't get any votes, cross it out right away. Discuss the remaining ideas carefully, examining both pros and cons. Then choose the best idea.

4. Plan ways to try out your idea.

Treat this step of the process like a science experiment. Plan every step. Define how you will know whether or not the idea worked.

5. Put your plan into action.

Carry out each step of your plan. Involve all group members as actively as possible.

6. Re-evaluate.

Review your results. Is the problem solved? Or do you need to find another solution? If so, go back and repeat the same steps. Use what you learned from your first try to plan your second try.

Set Standards

If the group seems to be getting off track, it may help to stop and define some standards, or rules for appropriate behavior. Some groups adopt rules like the ones below. Your particular group may want to add other standards.

- Consider the volume. Keep it low.

- Speak in a respectful tone of voice.

- Be polite.

- Pay attention, and show that you're paying attention.

- Participate! Everyone needs to do his or her fair share.

Keep in mind that it is much easier to solve problems in a group when all members share ideas and respect each other's opinions.

Assign Jobs

One way to keep group members involved is to make sure everyone has a job and knows what it is. Below are some roles you can assign. You may need to assign other roles depending on the purpose of your group.

◆ Timekeeper

The timekeeper watches the clock and keeps everyone on track. Sometimes group members can get so involved in a discussion that they don't realize how quickly time is passing. It's the timekeeper's job to speak up when a part of the day's agenda has gone past its allotted time.

◆ Recorder

When group members get involved in a discussion, it's easy to forget what's been said before. And if any conflicts arise, it's nice to know exactly what each member said. The recorder takes detailed notes and reads back the notes at the group's request.

◆ Materials Handler

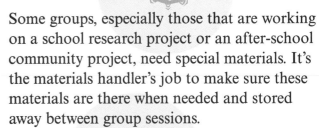

Some groups, especially those that are working on a school research project or an after-school community project, need special materials. It's the materials handler's job to make sure these materials are there when needed and stored away between group sessions.

◆ Reporter(s)

If the group is working on a research project, one or more members may be called on to share the results with the rest of the class. Reporters should be prepared to present the group's work in a concise and organized manner.

◆ Discussion Leader

If the group is a large one, you may need to appoint someone to keep the discussion on track. The leader makes sure everyone gets to speak and asks the recorder to read back the notes when necessary.

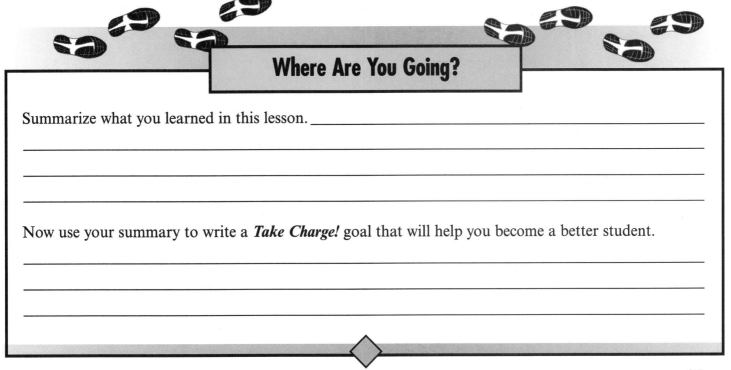

Where Are You Going?

Summarize what you learned in this lesson. _____

_____

_____

_____

Now use your summary to write a *Take Charge!* goal that will help you become a better student.

_____

_____

_____

LESSON 9

Scheduling Study Time

Meet Joe

Believe it or not, Joe is usually happy and easygoing. His friends know him as the guy who likes to make plans at the last minute and somehow finds a way to "get by" in his school-work. Joe doesn't seem to take anything very seriously.

So why does Joe look so unhappy? He just discovered that a laid-back approach isn't always the best strategy, especially when it comes to preparing for tests. Joe spent some time studying the night before the big social studies test, but it was too little, too late. No wonder he isn't happy with his grade!

Where Do You Stand?

Read how Joe spent the three nights before his test. Cross out and rewrite parts of the schedule to help Joe do a better job of studying for his test.

Tuesday

3:30–5:00	Play ball with friends
5:00–6:00	Listen to new disc while doing homework
6:00–6:30	Eat dinner
6:30–7:30	Talk on the phone
7:30–9:45	Watch a movie

Wednesday

3:30–4:00	Piano lesson
4:00–6:00	Watch soccer game at school
6:00–6:30	Eat dinner
6:30–8:00	Play video game at friend's
8:00–9:45	Watch TV while doing homework

Thursday

3:30–4:30	After-school club meeting
4:30–6:00	Call friends to talk and ask what's on tomorrow's test
6:00–7:00	Eat dinner; clean up kitchen
7:00–8:00	Help Mom with groceries
8:00–9:00	Watch TV while doing homework
9:00–9:45	Cram for test

Plan a Study Strategy

Use the calendar below to plan a week of special study sessions for an upcoming test. Schedule at least one study session each day. Think about all the ways you know to study for a test. Do you like to work with a friend? Recopy your notes? Make flash cards? Allow time in your schedule for all your favorite study methods. Before you begin, read *Scheduling Secrets* in the next column. They'll help you make a test-prep plan that really works!

Scheduling Secrets

◆ Schedule fixed time blocks first, such as your class schedule.

◆ Determine what other time blocks are available for possible study time.

◆ Set realistic time estimates for study time during these time blocks.

◆ Set clear starting and stopping times.

◆ Schedule time for short breaks.

◆ Be sure to schedule some time for fun each day.

	Monday —/—/—	Tuesday —/—/—	Wednesday —/—/—	Thursday —/—/—	Friday —/—/—
7:00					
8:00					
9:00					
10:00					
11:00					
12:00					
1:00					
2:00					
3:00					
4:00					
5:00					
6:00					
7:00					
8:00					
9:00					
10:00					

Tips for Scheduling Study Time

Plan Ahead

Postponing your studying until the day before the test is like preparing for an athletic competition by exercising for one day. If you haven't been working out all along, you're not in shape, and one day's exercise won't help. The way to make sure you're in tip-top test-taking shape is to manage your time to allow for daily study and review.

Review your notes every day, whether there's a test coming up or not. Make sure your daily schedule allows at least fifteen minutes to review each of your subjects. Divide your daily reviews into two parts. Use half of your review time to reread information you've learned in the last day or week. Use the rest of your time to memorize facts like names, dates, definitions, and equations.

You can't push back the hands of time. Make sure you are ready for tests by scheduling daily study and review. Begin your serious studying four or five days before a test.

Ready, Set, Study!

DAY 1

On the first day, just skim your notes, homework assignments, and quizzes. Look for gaps in the information. If you find any, fill them in by reading your textbook or asking your teacher or a classmate for help.

DAY 2

On the second day, skim all the test material. Recite important ideas out loud to yourself and make sure you can explain each idea clearly.

DAY 3

On the third day, read over your notes. Write key words and ideas in the margins. Make flash cards. Then, without looking at the rest of your notes, say aloud to yourself the details that go with each key word or main idea.

DAY 4

On the fourth day, use your notes to make up a sample test and test yourself, or have someone quiz you on your notes. If you're doing well at this point, give yourself a short break. If you don't do so well on your practice test, repeat the quizzing process until you're sure you understand all the important ideas and have memorized the facts you need to know to explain the ideas. Practice tests will make the real thing feel like no big deal.

The Pros and Cons of Cramming

You may hear some people say that they never study until the night before a test. Trying to get all your studying done in one marathon study session is called "cramming." If you think cramming is a good idea, read the Pros and Cons below. Then decide for yourself.

PROS:

◆ You stuff a lot of studying into a little bit of time.

◆ You might pass the test.

CONS:

◆ You'll probably forget what you studied as soon as the test is over.

◆ You won't have the knowledge base you'll need to learn new things in the future.

◆ You're likely to feel stressed and nervous on the day of the test.

◆ All the time you spent in class was wasted.

◆ You might not pass the test.

Three, Two, One, Test Time!

Start getting psyched up for a big test on the night before. Review the material you've been studying for the past several days and then relax and get a good night's sleep. In the morning, eat a good breakfast, do a little exercise to get your blood flowing, and take a shower to get your brain in gear. If you have time, go over the material briefly once again. Put on some comfortable clothes, gather everything you'll need for the test, and say to yourself, "I'm a winner!"

Get to class early. On your way to the classroom, go to the restroom and get a drink of water. Get comfortable in your seat and settle in. Clear your desk of unnecessary items, sit straight up in your chair, and take a few deep breaths. Then relax until the test begins—you're ready for success!

Assess Yourself

Look back at the schedule you planned on page 37. Now that you've studied these tips, are there any changes you'd like to make? If so, make the adjustments now.

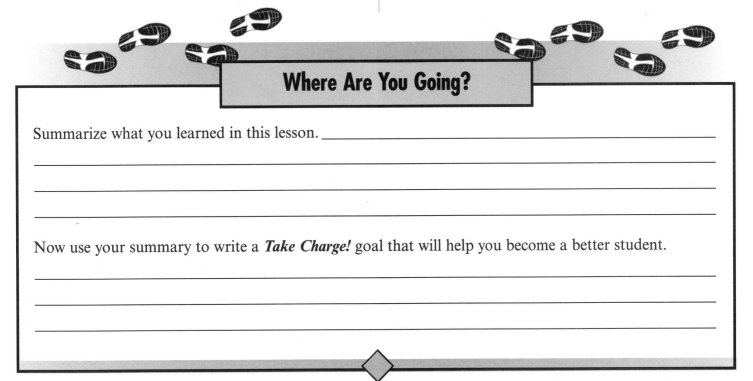

Where Are You Going?

Summarize what you learned in this lesson. _____

_____

_____

_____

Now use your summary to write a *Take Charge!* goal that will help you become a better student.

_____

_____

_____

LESSON 10

Monitoring Your Test Readiness

I thought I knew this.

Do You Know What You Know?

As you study for tests, do you feel that you have a pretty good idea of what you understand and what you need to spend more time on? Knowing how well you're doing is called *self-monitoring*. It means keeping track of your own progress.

Successful students monitor their progress while they study. This helps them decide what steps to take next—whether to go over difficult material again, try a different study strategy, or ask for help. Some students monitor themselves automatically, but those who don't can learn how.

Where Do You Stand?

How good are you at self-monitoring your test readiness? Complete the questionnaire below to find out. Read the statements and think about what you do when you have a test. Fill in the circle that shows how often you do each thing.

1. I feel confident while I'm taking a test.

| Hardly Ever | ① | ② | ③ | ④ | ⑤ | Almost Always |

2. During class and when I'm studying, I ask myself questions to make sure I understand the material.

| Hardly Ever | ① | ② | ③ | ④ | ⑤ | Almost Always |

3. As I study, I stop periodically to test myself.

| Hardly Ever | ① | ② | ③ | ④ | ⑤ | Almost Always |

4. I make checklists to make sure I haven't forgotten anything.

| Hardly Ever | ① | ② | ③ | ④ | ⑤ | Almost Always |

5. I use different methods—such as flash cards or revising my notes—to study different kinds of information.

| Hardly Ever | ① | ② | ③ | ④ | ⑤ | Almost Always |

6. I review tests I've taken to find ways I could have improved my scores.

| Hardly Ever | ① | ② | ③ | ④ | ⑤ | Almost Always |

Rate Yourself

To rate your skills, add up the numbers in the circles you filled in. Write your total in the box.

◆ If you scored over 24, congratulations! You already use some self-monitoring as you study.

◆ If you scored between 15 and 23, you sometimes monitor your own test readiness, but you can become more aware of what you do and don't know.

◆ If you scored below 15, you may have trouble knowing when you're ready for a test. By learning to monitor your test readiness, you'll be a more successful and confident test-taker.

Are You Ready?

Aggh! One of your teachers just announced that in two weeks there will be a review test over everything you have studied in class so far this year. How will you prepare?

Get together with two or three others who have the same class as you. Look through your textbook and notes and brainstorm some facts you might find on a review test for that class. Then fill in the chart below. In the top, write sample facts you might find on the test—some facts you think you already know and some you need to learn. In the lower part, write some ways you might review or learn those facts for the test. Use the study strategies at right for some ideas.

Facts I Think I Know	Facts I Don't Know
Study Strategies	**Study Strategies**

Study Strategies
- flash cards
- revise/recopy notes
- study group
- outlines, webs, and graphic organizers
- mnemonic devices
- practice tests
- recite out loud
- checklists

Tips for Monitoring Yourself

Review, Review, Review

You'll always be ready for a quiz or a test if you constantly review. Don't just read over your notes and stop. Analyze what you know and don't know. Ask yourself whether you could explain the main ideas to someone who has never heard them before. See which facts and details you can rattle off without taking time to think about them. Make a list of things you still don't understand. Then reread your notes and textbook or ask questions. When you feel confident about your knowledge, cross the item off your list.

Test Yourself

Every once in a while, stop to make up a sample test for yourself. Try to make it as much like the tests your teacher gives as possible. Create questions that test your knowledge of main ideas and details and questions that force you to make connections and apply what you've learned. Then take your self-made test to see how you're doing.

Join Study Groups

If you're the kind of person who likes to study with friends, you already know how useful the give-and-take between members of a study group can be. But even if you usually prefer studying alone, studying occasionally with a group can give you some useful guidelines for monitoring your test readiness. You can measure your progress against that of other group members on a regular basis. And you and the other members of the group can help each other out—after all, everyone has different weaknesses and strengths.

Try having each group member write some questions about different sections of the material, or have everyone in the group write a sample test for the whole group to take. Work together to decide what the group members need to learn at the next study session.

When forming a study group, remember that it is important to keep all members involved. Be respectful of everyone in the group and you will benefit from each other's ideas.

Check It Off

Make a checklist for each subject. Then, as you prepare to take a test, use your checklist the way astronauts use preflight checklists before blasting off. After all, as every astronaut knows, once you're in space it's too late to correct something you forgot to check. Your pretest checklist can help you monitor yourself. You can see whether you've prepared for every kind of question that might appear on the test.

Begin your checklists on the very first day of class and add to them as the year goes on. Include page numbers of reading assignments, dates of class notes, problems you'll need to solve, and skills you'll have to master. Include major ideas, definitions, theories, formulas, and equations as separate items on your checklists. When it comes time to prepare for a big test, check each item off the list as you master it.

Live and Learn

When your teacher returns your corrected test, don't just take a quick peek at the grade, groan, and hide the test away somewhere. Take a close look at it with these questions in mind:

◆ What kinds of questions did my teacher ask? Which kind gave me the most trouble?

◆ What material did the test focus on—class notes, textbooks, or homework exercises? Was it the material I concentrated on as I studied?

◆ What did I do best on the test?

◆ What study strategies helped me the most?

◆ What changes do I need to make to do better the next time?

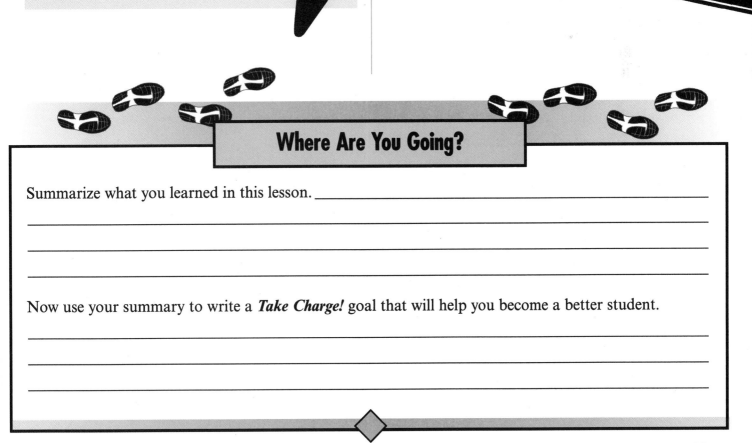

Where Are You Going?

Summarize what you learned in this lesson. _____

_____

_____

_____

Now use your summary to write a *Take Charge!* goal that will help you become a better student.

_____

_____

_____

Techniques for Memorizing

One of the most famous speakers in ancient Rome was Cicero. Cicero used a special trick to remember his speeches.

Memory Matters

How did the famous Roman orator Cicero remember his speeches? He didn't use index cards or TelePrompTers. Cicero associated parts of his speeches with parts of his home. The opening of the speech might have been linked with his bed chamber, the next part with his yard. As he progressed through the speech, Cicero mentally took a walk through the rooms in his house.

Succeeding in school depends on remembering things like dates, math and science formulas, historical events, characters, and plots. There are two basic ways to memorize. One is by repetition—reading or saying something over and over until you know it "by heart." The other is what Cicero did—linking new ideas to something familiar. You can link what you're trying to remember with images and words that are so silly you just can't forget them or with images and words that are already familiar. Learning new strategies for making memory links will save you time when you memorize. It can even be fun!

Where Do You Stand?

You probably already use memory links, or *mnemonic* (ni MON ik) *devices*. Do the words and phrases below look familiar? Each one is a mnemonic device. Write an explanation for each one that you know.

1. HOMES

_____

_____

_____

2. When two vowels go walking, the first vowel does the talking.

_____

_____

_____

3. My Uncle Steve can lift elephants.

_____

_____

_____

4. My very excellent mother just served us nine pizzas.

_____

_____

_____

Rate Yourself

Read the answers to see how you did. If some of the memory links were unfamiliar, use them now to remember the facts.

1. HOMES is an acronym that helps us remember that the five Great Lakes are Huron, Ontario, Michigan, Erie, and Superior.

2. When you were just beginning to read, you may have learned this rhyme to remember that the first vowel in a pair is usually the one you pronounce. Can you think of an example?

3. This sentence helps you remember how to spell the word *muscle*.

4. This sentence helps you list the planets in our solar system in order of distance from the sun: Mercury, Venus, Earth, Mars, Jupiter, Saturn, Uranus, Neptune, Pluto.

Think Like Cicero

Remember Cicero's memory trick? He pictured a familiar place and put one thing he wanted to remember in each room. Try the same idea to remember a nonsense list. Picture the items on the list below in different places in your school. Then cover the list, take an imaginary walk, and write what you remember on the lines below.

giraffe, lake, pencil, daisy, automobile, mountain, football, book, tree, fence

_____

_____

_____

_____

How Do You Spell It?

Some words are just plain confusing. You could practice spelling them over and over and still make a mistake. Mnemonic devices, or memory links, can help you. Here are a few examples of memory tricks for spelling.

principal (of your school)—The principal is my pal.

principle—The principle is the rule.

acquaint—I will seek you (CQ) out to get acquainted.

bargain—You gain from a bargain.

There are many other troublesome words. Here are some examples:

separate	comfortable	occur
address	bureau	foreign
potatoes	commitment	environment

Work with a small group of classmates to create memory links for three of the troublesome words above. Write your ideas below.

_____

_____

_____

_____

_____

_____

_____

_____

Add Memory Power

Make a Link

You've learned that memorizing works best when you associate an unfamiliar idea with something you already know. The sillier or more unusual your association is, the easier it will be to remember the new idea. For example, suppose you need to remember that *prostar* is the beginning stage in the cycle of the development of a star. You might think, *This rookie is going to be a star in the pros someday* and draw a picture of a basketball player dunking a star in the basket.

Try it for yourself. Make up an image to help you remember the fact that George Washington Carver developed hundreds of industrial uses for southern crops like sweet potatoes and peanuts. Draw a picture in the space below.

Make Up an Acronym

Acronyms are words that are made up of the initials of other words. HOMES is an example of an acronym. If you can create a word (or words) from the first letter of each word on a list you need to memorize, you'll always be able to recall that list.

Make Up a Saying

If you can't make up an acronym, you might find it easier to make up a saying. Catchy sayings stick in your mind. For example, *Spring forward, fall back* tells you when to set the clock ahead an hour and when to set it back for daylight savings time. You can add a mental picture to make your saying stand out even more.

Make Sentences

Create humorous sentences whose words begin with the same letters as the names of the items you're memorizing. <u>S</u>illy <u>M</u>illy <u>h</u>ates <u>e</u>ating <u>o</u>nions is another way to remember the names of the Great Lakes. You can use the sentence when you need to place the Great Lakes on a map from west to east: Superior, Michigan, Huron, Erie, Ontario. Practice this technique by making up a sentence to help you memorize the last five presidents of the United States, in order. Write your sentence on the lines below.

_____

_____

_____

_____

_____

_____

_____

_____

Make a Rhyme or Sing a Song

Rhymes such as *In fourteen hundred ninety-two, Columbus sailed the ocean blue* are easy to remember. They make facts easy to remember, too. You may have learned to sing the rhyme instead of just saying it. Singing information you need to remember, even if it doesn't rhyme, is another good memory trick. It works especially well if you use a tune you already know.

Try this spelling rhyme to help you remember how to spell some troublesome words.

> Write **i** before **e**
> Except after **c**
> Or when sounded like **a**
> As in **neighbor** and **weigh**.
> **Weird, their,** and **neither**
> Aren't the same **either**.

Memorizing Tips

◆ Memorize at the beginning of your study time, when you're most alert. Memorizing gets harder as you get tired.

◆ Be sure you understand the material before you try to memorize it.

◆ Write down the things you need to memorize.

◆ Talk to yourself. Say aloud the words you need to memorize.

◆ Make a connection. Link new material to facts you already know.

Hint:
Mnemonic devices aren't *always* necessary and should be reserved for information that is particularly difficult for you to remember!

Where Are You Going?

Summarize what you learned in this lesson. _____

_____

_____

_____

Now use your summary to write a ***Take Charge!*** goal that will help you become a better student.

_____

_____

_____

Understanding Test Formats

You've passed lots of tests in your life, and you'll need to pass even more.

Test Time

You've already taken lots of tests in your life as a student, and you're sure to be taking many more, both in and out of school. You need to take tests to pass your classes, to get your driver's license, to get into college or technical school, and maybe even to get a job. Different types of tests are designed to find out different things. Therefore, it's very important to understand the purpose of a test. When you know the purpose, you have a better chance of giving correct answers.

Where Do You Stand?

An attitude inventory is designed to help you understand your feelings and preferences. Think about the kinds of questions on the tests you take. Then answer the questions in this attitude inventory.

1. What kind of question—true-false, multiple-choice, matching, short-answer, or essay—do you think is the easiest? Why? _____ _____ _____

2. What kind of test question do you think is the hardest? Why? _____ _____

3. Which kind of test question do you usually do well on? Why? _____ _____

4. What would you do to change the way tests are given? _____ _____ _____

5. What ways besides tests can you think of to assess student progress? _____ _____

Understand Every Test's Purpose

Different kinds of tests have different purposes. Listed below are five types of tests you will probably encounter. Read the descriptions of each test. Understanding what a test can mean to you gives you an incentive to study and perform your best.

- **Classroom tests** measure how much you've learned in a few days or weeks, a school term, or an entire school year. Because classroom tests occur so often, they help you know where you stand in your classes and what you need to study.

- **Standardized tests, or norm-referenced tests,** compare achievement level with a statistical sample of other students. These tests let you know where you rank in a group of students your age from all over the United States who have taken the same test.

- **Criterion-referenced tests** measure what you know without comparing you with other students. They tell you which skills you've mastered and which ones you still need to work on. If you take a state proficiency test, it's probably a criterion-referenced test.

- **Aptitude tests** analyze your skills, abilities, and interests. When it's time for you to choose a career, an aptitude test can help you learn what type of work you might be good at and what you might enjoy.

- **Entrance exams** measure your qualification for admission to special programs or schools.

Test Talk

In a small group, review the five types of tests and their purposes. Then work together to think of examples of each kind of test you've taken. Describe them on the lines below.

1. Classroom test _____

_____

_____

2. Standardized test _____

_____

_____

3. Criterion-referenced test _____

_____

_____

4. Aptitude test _____

_____

_____

5. Entrance exam _____

_____

_____

6. Other tests _____

_____

_____

_____

Know Your Test Strategies

The following strategies will help you do your best on different types of test questions.

True-False

> Circle True or False.
>
> A quasar is a starlike object that gives off tremendous amounts of energy.
>
> **True**   **False**

◆ Remember that statements containing absolutes such as *never, always, all, every time,* and *none* are often false.

◆ Answer *true* right away if you're positive the statement is correct. If you're not sure, reread the question carefully and try to think of exceptions to the statement.

◆ It's easier to write a statement with one or more exceptions, or a false statement, than a true one. If you just don't know the answer, time is running out, and you need to make a guess, mark *false*.

Essay

> Explain the life cycle of a star.

◆ Read each question carefully, noting key words in the directions. Make sure you know exactly what kind of answer the question calls for.

◆ Begin by writing a short outline or web.

◆ Write your answer the same way you would write a longer essay or report—with an introduction, a well-organized main body, and a conclusion.

◆ Show what you know. Include plenty of details, examples, and specifics.

Analogy

> *Milky Way : galaxy :: Ursa Major : _____*

An analogy is a comparison. In an analogy question, one of the words is missing and you must fill it in.

◆ Read analogy questions as sentences even if they're not written that way. The example above is read *Milky Way is to galaxy as Ursa Major is to _____.*

◆ To complete an analogy, think of a way to describe the relationship between the first two words in the analogy. Then choose a word to complete the analogy so that the second pair of words show the same relationship as the first. In the example above, the completed analogy would read *Milky Way is to galaxy as Ursa Major is to constellation.*

Short-Answer

> *Complete this sentence.*
>
> A galaxy is a huge system, or family, of _____.

◆ To answer short-answer questions, you only write a word, number, name, or phrase. Many short-answer questions are incomplete sentences. Others are questions with a short writing line beside them.

◆ Don't look for hidden meanings in short-answer questions. Their purpose is simply to test your recall of key facts, words, and phrases.

◆ If you think there may be two correct answers, look to see how many lines follow the question. If there's only one short line, write the best answer.

Multiple-Choice

Fill in the bubble next to the correct answer that completes the sentence.

A light-year is the distance light travels in one year. It is equal to _____ kilometers.

- Ⓐ 9.46 trillion
- Ⓑ 9.46 billion
- Ⓒ 9.46 million
- Ⓓ 9.46 thousand

◆ Answer the questions you're sure about first.

◆ Follow your first instinct. Don't change an answer unless you have a good reason for believing you've made a mistake.

◆ Think carefully about *loners*. Loners are answer choices that are very different from the other choices in the group. Although loners are usually not the correct answer, they can sometimes surprise you.

Ready, Set, Go!

When you sit down to study for a test, do you get up again and again to find the things you need? Solve your organization problem by keeping a file folder for each class. In each file, place the papers you'll need when it's time for a test. Bring home everything that relates to the class—your tests and quizzes, homework assignments, and stories and research papers you've written. Take a few minutes every day to file these papers in the class folders. Store your file folders in a drawer, cabinet, or box in a place that's out of the reach of little brothers or sisters and pets. Do these things, and you'll be all ready to study when test time comes!

Where Are You Going?

Summarize what you learned in this lesson. _____

_____

_____

_____

Now use your summary to write a ***Take Charge!*** goal that will help you become a better student.

_____

_____

_____

Taking Short-Answer and Essay Tests

Words of Experience

Dear Testmaster,

Essay tests terrify me! True-false, multiple-choice, analogies, and even short-answer or fill-in-the-blank tests are a breeze. There are usually enough clues in the questions to help me remember the answers. But an essay test is too much like a blank sheet of paper. Not only do I have to know what I'm writing about, I also have to think of a way to write what I know in a clear and organized way. And all that in one class period! Is that fair?

Terrified in Toledo

Dear Terrified in Toledo,

Yes, it's fair. In fact, essay tests are the best way for you to show what you know. When you've studied hard, learned the information you need to know, and mastered the basic writing skills that you use for any writing assignment, you can relax. Essay tests won't be a problem. Don't be afraid of expressing your own ideas and opinions. Just remember to back up your thoughts with supporting facts and details that prove your point. Your teacher will know that you've mastered the information—and that you know how to think for yourself!

The Testmaster

Where Do You Stand?

Do you feel like Terrified in Toledo when your teacher announces a test with short-answer or essay questions on it? Relax! If you understand the purpose of these tests, it will help ease your fears about taking them. See how much you already know about essay and short-answer tests by taking the quiz below. Circle the correct answer.

1. Which type of test would best measure your knowledge of important names, dates, and events in history?

   a. essay test   **b.** short-answer test

2. Which type of test measures your ability to memorize your class notes and the highlights of your reading assignments?

   a. essay test   **b.** short-answer test

3. Which type of test would best measure your ability to analyze or compare things?

   a. essay test   **b.** short-answer test

4. Which type of test requires you to summarize key points about a topic?

   a. essay test   **b.** short-answer test

5. Which type of test usually requires you to complete a sentence correctly?

   a. essay test   **b.** short-answer test

Rate Yourself

Were all your answers correct? If so, you're well on your way to understanding how to conquer short-answer and essay tests. Read on to develop more test-taking strategies. If these types of tests are still a mystery to you, don't panic. This lesson will help you get on the right track.

How to Tackle Tests

What strategies do you use to study for essay and short-answer tests? Do you vary your study method when you know these types of questions will be on the tests?

Get together in a small group and discuss ways that each of you study differently for various tests. List your ideas below.

Study Strategies for Short-Answer Tests

_____

_____

_____

_____

_____

_____

_____

Study Strategies for Essay Tests

_____

_____

_____

_____

_____

_____

Plan an Essay

Did you know that the French word *essay* means "to try or attempt"? Read the four essay questions below. Give your best effort to plan an answer for one of the essay questions. Use the space to make a brief web or outline that shows what you would write.

1. *Summarize the roles of the three branches of the U.S. government: executive, legislative, and judicial.*

2. *Compare and contrast the Vietnam War and the Persian Gulf War.*

3. *Describe the way an invention you use every day works.*

4. *Explain the term* interdependence *as it relates to Earth's living things.*

Share your outline or web with a partner. Discuss similarities and differences and talk about how you would use your plans to write complete essays.

Tips for Answering Short-Answer and Essay Questions

Short-Answer Questions

To complete a short-answer test, you usually fill in blanks in incomplete sentences. You're not given any answers to choose from, so you need to generate the answer, or "pull it out of your mind." That means you have to have studied hard enough to have the answer in your mind in the first place!

The purpose of short-answer questions is to test your recall of key terms, facts, and details. If you memorize your class notes and the highlights of your reading assignments, you should have no problem recalling the answers to short-answer questions. Just in case you run into trouble, though, here are a few tips that may help:

◆ Reread the question several times.

◆ Watch for context clues in the question or in other questions on the test.

◆ Check to see if the word before the blank is *a* or *an*. If it's *an*, the correct answer begins with a vowel.

◆ Check the verb in the sentence. If it's singular, the answer must be singular. If it's plural, the answer must be plural.

◆ Answer the easy questions first. Then go back to the harder questions. The answers to some questions may help you recall the answers to others.

Story Problems

Story problems are a special kind of short-answer question. You'll often find them on math and science tests. To answer a story problem, you read a passage, analyze it to find the question or problem, determine the appropriate method for solving it, apply the method correctly, and express the answer in the correct form. If you're having difficulty with a story problem, ask yourself these questions:

◆ What exactly is the problem or question?

◆ What information is provided? Will I use all of it to answer the question?

◆ Can I make a diagram or picture to help me solve the problem?

◆ How have I answered similar questions in the past?

◆ What form should my answer take?

These questions will help you locate information in the story problem. Find the clues, write them down, translate them into symbols and sentences, and study them closely. Soon you will see the key to the problem. As you work out the problem, show all your steps and calculations clearly. Even if your answer is wrong, you may get partial credit if the method you used is correct.

Build your test-taking confidence by trying these tips.

Essay Questions

Essay answers may range from a few sentences to a few paragraphs in length. Your essay answer should be as carefully worded and well organized as a full-length essay or report. Use these strategies to write clear, thoughtful essay answers in a short amount of time:

♦ **Plan your time carefully.** It's easy to forget about time when you become engrossed in answering an essay question, but don't! Watch the clock and pace yourself accordingly. Be sure to allow time to answer all the questions on the test.

♦ **Know your facts.** Make sure you've prepared for the test thoroughly. That way you can concentrate on your writing rather than trying to think of something to say.

♦ **Start with an outline or web.** As with other writing assignments, start with a brief outline. Your outline will help you write your thoughts in logical order. And if you run out of time before you finish your answer, the outline or web will show your teacher where you were headed.

♦ **Write legibly.** Obviously, if your teacher can't read what you've written it won't count for much!

♦ **Use complete sentences.** Don't let the time limit rattle you. Write full sentences just as you ordinarily would. Use transition words, such as *first*, *second*, and *finally*, that clearly demonstrate how one thought logically follows another.

♦ **Rewrite the question in the form of a statement** and announce what you're going to write about in your opening paragraph. Use the main body of your answer to make your point. End your essay with a concluding paragraph that summarizes your main ideas.

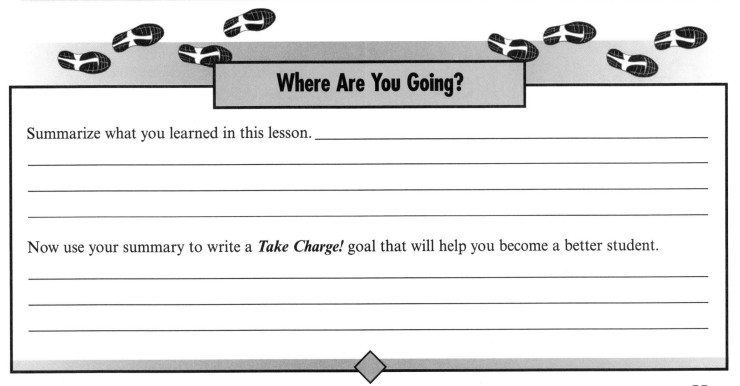

Where Are You Going?

Summarize what you learned in this lesson. _____

_____

_____

_____

Now use your summary to write a *Take Charge!* goal that will help you become a better student.

_____

_____

_____

Taking Multiple-Choice Tests

How do you feel about multiple-choice tests?

Multiple-choice tests are
Ⓐ easy for me.
Ⓑ trickier than short-answer tests.
Ⓒ harder than essay tests.

Choices, Choices...

Which answer did you choose? If you circled *b* or *c,* don't be discouraged. You can learn new test-taking strategies that will make multiple-choice tests easier. And it's important to master multiple-choice questions. Most standardized tests and many other school tests include multiple-choice questions. As you advance in school and the tests you take become more difficult, you'll be glad you took the time to learn the ABCs of multiple-choice tests.

Where Do You Stand?

Do you already use some good strategies when you take a multiple-choice test? Take this quiz to find out. Read each question carefully. Circle the letter of the best answer.

1. When taking a multiple-choice test, it's a good strategy to
   a. answer easy questions first.
   b. work through difficult questions as you come to them.
   c. skip easy questions and come back to them at the end.

2. When reading a multiple-choice test, it's best to
   a. study all the answer choices and then try to guess which one is correct.
   b. answer each question in your head first and then look at the answer choices.
   c. none of the above

3. If you think choice *a* is the correct answer,
   a. circle it and go quickly to the next question.
   b. read the rest of the answer choices anyway before making any marks.
   c. save time by not reading any of the other answer choices.

4. If you change an answer, be sure to
   a. erase the first answer completely.
   b. cross out the answer you want to change.
   c. none of the above

Rate Yourself

Now check your answers to see how you did.

1. a. The first time you go through a multiple-choice test, just answer the questions you're sure about. Come back to hard questions later. Otherwise, you might not leave enough time to answer the questions you know.

2. b. If you answer each question in your head before you look at the answer choices, you won't be confused by incorrect answers.

3. b. Don't get lured into choosing wrong answers that seem at first glance to be correct. Read over all the answer choices before making any marks.

4. a. If you change an answer, be sure to erase the first answer completely so the person—or machine—who scores your test won't be confused.

Educated Guesses

Although there are tips and special strategies for taking multiple-choice tests, you have to study. You need to know the test material in order to make an educated guess. Sometimes, for example, you can narrow the choices down to two answers. But it is your knowledge that helps you choose the correct response.

With a partner, answer this question. Be prepared to explain how you made your choice.

> Complete this sentence.
>
> The Trojan Horse was full of _____ .
>
> a. Greek soldiers
>
> b. gifts
>
> c. boiling oil
>
> d. Trojan soldiers

Tricky Tests

With a partner, discuss the following situations. Decide how each student could improve his or her test-taking skills. Write your conclusions on the lines.

Situation 1: Jake answered the following question incorrectly.

> Choose the word that means the opposite of the given word.
>
> synthetic
>
> a. expensive   c. natural
>
> (b.) unreal   d. manufactured

Jake answered *b*. What's the correct answer? Why do you think Jake got the wrong answer?

_____

_____

_____

Situation 2: Rachel answered the following question incorrectly.

> Circle the best answer.
>
> What is the amount of an American coin that is greater in value than a dime (10¢)?
>
> (a.) 11¢   c. 20¢
>
> b. 15¢   d. 25¢

Rachel answered *a*. What's the correct answer? Why do you think Rachel chose *a*?

_____

_____

_____

Hints for Taking Multiple-Choice Tests

Multiple-Choice Tests for Reading

◆ When you answer multiple-choice questions about a reading passage, read the questions before you read the selection. That way, you'll know what to look for as you read the passage.

◆ Questions about factual details often ask about the *Five Ws—Who, What, When, Where,* and *Why.* You can get a head start if you look for details that answer these questions as you read.

◆ If you know about the subject of the selection, don't assume that you can answer questions from your prior knowledge. Look back at the selection to find support for your answers.

Multiple-Choice Tests for Math

◆ Read each question carefully to find out what you need to do. Then reread it to find the specific information you need to solve the problem.

◆ Before you read the answer choices, estimate what you think the answer will be.

◆ Work out math problems in the margins, on the back of the test, or on scrap paper. Draw pictures, charts, or tables if they will help you.

◆ For a measurement or geometry problem, first write down the formula you need to solve the problem. Then plug in the numbers from the problem.

Watch Out for Negative Words!

Be aware of negative words such as *not* or *opposite* in questions or directions. It's easy to skip over these words when you're nervous or in a hurry. If you don't read the question slowly and carefully, you may find yourself choosing the answer that is exactly the opposite of the correct one.

Is Anything ALWAYS True?

Watch out for questions or answer choices that include words such as *all, none, always, never,* and *every.* Very few absolute statements are true in every possible case. If one of the words above appears in a question or answer, think hard. Try to find an exception to the statement.

Does Long Equal Correct?

With multiple-choice responses, the longest, most complicated and carefully written answer may be correct because of the detailed information that is included. This is not an absolute rule, but a general principle to keep in mind. Rereading the longest answer is a good place to start when you're unsure of the correct answer.

Forget About Patterns

Don't even bother to look for a pattern in the answers. Most teachers and test-makers know that students often do this, so they usually check to make sure no pattern exists. They may even try to trick you by making one letter correct more often than others or by using a letter only one or two times—or not at all. Don't expect that you'll be marking the same number of *a*'s, *b*'s, *c*'s, and *d*'s.

DOs

- DO read all the directions carefully. Never start answering any of the questions until you've read the directions.

- DO mark the answer sheet carefully. If you skip a question because it's difficult, be sure to skip the corresponding number on the answer sheet. Each time you mark an answer, check to see that you have written it in the answer space that has the same number as the question.

- DO check your answers if you have time at the end of the test.

DON'Ts

- Don't hurry! It won't matter how quickly you complete a test if your answers aren't correct.

- Don't try to impress the teacher and other students by handing in the test early. Use extra time to review your answers. Spot-check the answer sheet to see that all numbers have only one answer filled in and all answers you changed have been erased completely.

- Don't leave an answer blank, especially if you can eliminate one or more incorrect choices. If you're not sure about an answer, use clues in the question to make an educated guess.

Where Are You Going?

Summarize what you learned in this lesson. _____

_____

_____

_____

Now use your summary to write a *Take Charge!* goal that will help you become a better student.

_____

_____

_____

Coping With Test Stress

It's hard not to worry on the day of the BIG TEST.

Don't Worry, Be Happy

Don't Worry, Be Happy is a good title for a song, but it's hard advice for many people to follow. It's natural to worry and feel anxious about important events like big tests. And a little stress isn't a bad thing. Stress can motivate you to work and study harder and to perform your best. But overwhelming anxiety can interfere with your ability to focus. Learning how to reduce anxiety and cope with stress can make important events more comfortable. It can even improve your test scores!

Where Do You Stand?

How much do you already know about coping with test stress? Take the following quiz to find out. Circle *True* or *False* to answer each question.

1. Stress affects you both physically and mentally.

| True | False |

2. Adrenaline is a stress hormone.

| True | False |

3. Stress makes your heart pump more blood and decreases your breathing rate.

| True | False |

4. Sweaty palms can result from stress.

| True | False |

5. One way to cope with stress is to breathe shallowly from your abdomen.

| True | False |

Rate Yourself

Check your answers to see how much you know about stress.

1. **True**—Stress can increase your heart rate, raise your blood pressure, and make your muscles tense. It can also slow your thinking process and make you irritable and depressed.

2. **True**—When you're anxious, your nervous system produces stress hormones, including adrenaline.

3. **False**—Stress increases your breathing rate, causing more oxygen to be sent to your larger muscles.

4. **True**—When you're under stress, sweat glands become activated to protect your body from becoming overheated.

5. **False**—One way to relax and cope with stress is to breathe deeply from your abdomen. If you breathe shallowly, you may not get enough oxygen. Taking rapid shallow breaths can lead to hyperventilation.

Calming Ideas

With a partner, brainstorm ways to cope with test stress. Then, using a separate sheet of paper, work together to write an acrostic poem to help you remember some of the methods you discussed. Use one letter of a word like *calm* or *stress* to begin each line of your poem. Share your poems with the class.

Study effectively
Take deep breaths
Relax your muscles
Exercise daily
Sleep eight hours at night
Stay confident

Challenge Irrational Thoughts

If you're a person who experiences test anxiety, some of the irrational thoughts below may sound familiar.

Imagine that a classmate has come to you and voiced these thoughts. On the lines below each statement, write the argument you would use to talk your friend out of the discouraging thought. Share your ideas with the class. Then, the next time you have a similar thought before a test, you can turn back to this page and reread your argument.

1. It doesn't matter how hard I study. I still won't do well on this test.

   _____

   _____

2. I'm the worst student in my class.

   _____

   _____

3. What if I'm so nervous I can't remember any of the answers?

   _____

   _____

4. No matter how hard I study, I'm just not smart enough to do well on this test.

   _____

   _____

5. I'd rather stay home sick than go to school and take the test.

   _____

   _____

Coping With Stress

Relax Your Muscles

One way to cope with stress is to learn to relax your body. When you're anxious, your muscles tighten and store tension. You can learn to drain tension from your body. You do this by tightening all your muscles beyond their normal tension point and then suddenly releasing the tension.

Try it for yourself. Sit or lie in a comfortable position in a quiet place. Close your eyes. Clench both hands tightly, making them into fists. Hold the tightness for seven seconds. Then let go. You can feel your tension being released.

Then squinch up your entire face as though you're trying to fit every part of it onto your nose. Hold the position for seven seconds and then release the tension. Repeat this same exercise with different muscle groups, such as your neck, shoulders, back, stomach, legs, and feet.

It may look funny, but squinching the muscles in your face and then relaxing them can help relieve tension.

Exercise Your Smile

There's another way to exercise the muscles in your face, and it's something you probably do often. You can exercise your face by using your muscles to smile. Smiling and laughing are two great ways to release tension. The harder you laugh, the more tension you release!

Is there a joke or mental picture that never fails to make you laugh? If so, you're ahead of the game. If not, maybe you need to rearrange your attitude to focus on things that are positive or funny. This is easier to do when you're already in a silly mood. When you're relaxed, think of things that make you laugh. Write them in a journal or commit them to memory. Then, next time you feel tense, open your journal or your mind, and pull out a memory that will help you smile and relax.

If laughter isn't the best medicine, it sure can't hurt!

Avoid Cramming

When you prepare for a test by cramming, you memorize a lot of information in a short period of time. Usually you retain this information for a very short time, too. When you cram, you feel as though you're under increased pressure. Your anxiety level rises even higher than normal. But feeling anxious means you are more likely to make mistakes on a test. If you experience test-taking anxiety, you should definitely plan ahead to avoid cramming.

Last-minute cramming for a test only increases your anxiety level.

Be Prepared!

"Be prepared" is good advice when you're getting ready to take a test or quiz. If you listen and take notes in class, schedule enough study time, and use your time wisely, you will feel prepared and confident when you sit down to take a test. And if you haven't prepared, no amount of relaxation exercises or positive thinking will keep you from feeling nervous.

Think like an Olympic athlete. You often hear athletes say, "I'm just here to have fun." What they mean is that they've done all the preparation they possibly can. When the time comes to perform, they give their best performance by relaxing and doing what they've proven they can do in practice thousands of times.

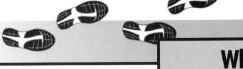

Where Are You Going?

Summarize what you learned in this lesson. _____

_____

_____

_____

Now use your summary to write a *Take Charge!* goal that will help you become a better student.

_____

_____

_____

Picturing Success

What is this gymnast thinking?

Go for the Gold!

Do you think the gymnast is picturing herself staying firmly on the balance beam through the end of her routine? Or do you think she's picturing herself falling to the ground with a big thump? If she's picturing success, she's likely to succeed. If she's picturing a fall, it will probably happen.

The best athletes use mental pictures to boost their scores. Before they perform, they picture exactly what they will do. While performing, they picture themselves succeeding. Making mental pictures is an important skill for athletes. It's an important skill for students, too.

Where Do You Stand?

How well do you use mental pictures to get yourself through your day? Find out by taking the quiz below. Read the statements. Fill in the circle that shows how often you do each thing.

1. When I'm worried about whether or not I'll be able to do something, I picture myself succeeding.

| Hardly Ever | ① | ② | ③ | ④ | ⑤ | Almost Always |

2. When I read directions, I picture myself going through each step.

| Hardly Ever | ① | ② | ③ | ④ | ⑤ | Almost Always |

3. Before I begin a new project, I imagine what the end product will look like.

| Hardly Ever | ① | ② | ③ | ④ | ⑤ | Almost Always |

4. When I listen to someone, I form mental pictures of what he or she is saying.

| Hardly Ever | ① | ② | ③ | ④ | ⑤ | Almost Always |

5. When I think of a place, such as a forest or a seashore, I can clearly see it in my mind's eye.

| Hardly Ever | ① | ② | ③ | ④ | ⑤ | Almost Always |

Rate Yourself

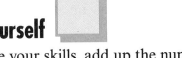

To rate your skills, add up the numbers in the circles you filled in. Write your total in the box.

- If you scored 20 or more, congratulations! You probably understand the importance of mental pictures.

- If you scored between 15 and 19, you know something about the technique. Using it consistently should help you succeed.

- If you scored below 15, try forming mental pictures. You may see a rapid improvement in your schoolwork and your attitude.

Practice Mental Pictures

With a partner, talk about activities you want to succeed in, such as taking a test, performing in a music or sports event, or mastering a new type of math problem. Describe pictures you could hold in your mind to improve your performance in these activities. On the chart below, list three of the activities. Then write descriptions of the mental pictures you think will help you succeed.

Activity	Mental Picture

Use Mental Pictures

As you read the story excerpt below, try to form mental images of the characters and setting. Then answer the questions.

I waited for Lori at the playground where we agreed to meet. It was weird, because she and I spent a lot of time here, once. I thought of her on a cold day at recess, jacket unzipped, hair flying. She ran with ease in a complicated path around the yard. Like a bee hovering over flowers, she stopped to ask one group of kids to join a game, to tell another group some dumb kid joke, or to lobby the teacher on recess duty for five more minutes of play time. Lori never walked. She needed me to help her, though. I helped her with math, and with her family, which was a little on the mixed-up side. That was years ago, two years since I had even talked to her. But today I needed her help. Boy, did I need help. The playground was empty, desolate. When would she get here?

1. Describe the most vivid mental picture you were able to form.

_____

_____

2. List three words that describe your mental picture of the playground.

_____

_____

3. In the space below, draw a picture that illustrates the story.

All About Mental Pictures

Hold On to Your Talent

When you were a young child, you probably formed mental pictures all the time without realizing it. All human beings are born with the ability to visualize, and most people keep that ability through their early teen years. But almost half of all adults in our culture lose the ability to form mental pictures—they simply forget how. This happens in spite of the fact that our culture places a high value on creativity, imagination, and intuition—all of which are based on the ability to form mental pictures.

Forming mental pictures adds interest to the things you read and hear. Your mental pictures will make faraway places and long ago events seem more real to you. The fact is that visualization is an extremely important learning tool. Mental pictures can help you remember important details and solve complex problems. Are you still able to form mental pictures easily? Remember that visualizing is a special talent. Read on to find out how you can hold on to your visualizing skills—and make them even better.

Give Yourself 20/20 Inner Vision

Some people who grew up before television was invented will tell you that listening to radio was more fun than watching television is today. That, they say, is because they had to make up pictures to go along with the stories they heard, and their mental pictures were usually better than the real thing. These same people may no longer have the ability to visualize. They don't have to visualize anymore, since television provides all the pictures they need. Without practice, they lost some of their talent.

You don't need to give up television to develop your talent for making mental pictures. Visualization is a skill that can be improved with practice. Here's a simple way to begin improving your visualization skills. Find a quiet spot where you can get comfortable and relax. Close your eyes, take a few deep breaths. Then tell yourself to picture a circle. Wait a few moments, and a circle should come floating into "view." Keep practicing with simple shapes like circles, squares, and triangles. Then move on to more complicated images—street scenes, a view from the top of a mountain, or the sun setting over the ocean. At first, picture familiar places. Then move on to imaginary scenes. Keep practicing. Soon your mental pictures will be as good as the ones you see on TV.

Do you form a mental picture in your mind of succeeding before beginning a task?

Listening With Pictures

The next time you're listening in class, try adding your own mental pictures. As your teacher speaks, try picturing what he or she is saying in your mind's eye. If the subject is a Civil War battle, for example, put yourself in the thick of the action. See the smoke from the gun barrels, hear the roar of the cannons. If the subject is how plants get nutrients from the soil, visualize water from the soil carrying nutrients into the plant's roots and up its stem to the leaves. But make sure you know the difference between visualizing and daydreaming. The helpful kind of visualizing is all about listening closely and actively to what the speaker has to say. It helps you remember what you hear.

Step-by-Step Directions

Making mental pictures can help you follow directions, too. Whether you're building a model, working on a project, writing a research report, or just doing your homework, mentally rehearsing the steps can help you get it right the first time. As you read the directions, imagine yourself going through every step. If you come to a point where you're not sure what to do next, or if you think you've done something wrong, reread the directions and retrace your steps. When you've pictured yourself walking through all the steps and completing the project perfectly, you're ready to begin the project for real.

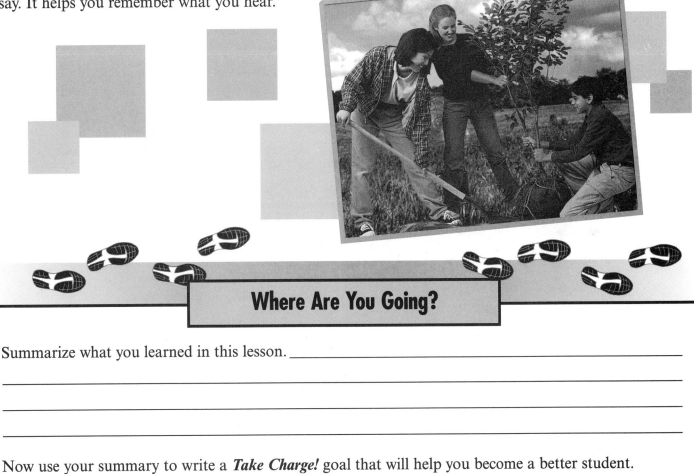

Where Are You Going?

Summarize what you learned in this lesson. _____

_____

_____

_____

Now use your summary to write a **_Take Charge!_** goal that will help you become a better student.

_____

_____

_____

Asking and Answering Questions

A Cliché That's True

The only stupid question is the one you don't ask.

No one knows who originated this often-heard cliché. Chances are it was a teacher. Clichés are phrases you should usually avoid—they're tired, overused expressions. But the strange thing about clichés is that they can be true.

Have you ever avoided asking a question because you thought everyone else knew the answer? Have you ever been afraid people would think your question was "dumb"? If so, you've probably learned the hard way that "the only stupid question is the one you don't ask."

Where Do You Stand?

See where you stand on the question of questions. Circle the letter of the answer that best expresses how you usually respond.

1. If you think of a question while your teacher is speaking, you usually
   a. go ahead and say it right out loud.
   b. raise your hand and wait to be called on.
   c. jot down your question and ask it after your teacher has finished.
   d. say nothing and hope someone else asks your question.

2. If your teacher asks you a question and you don't know the answer, you usually
   a. say nothing.
   b. make something up.
   c. admit that you don't know.
   d. pretend you didn't hear.

3. If you don't understand the answer to a question, you usually
   a. pretend that you do.
   b. ask for clarification.
   c. look it up in the encyclopedia.
   d. nod your head wisely.

4. If you have a question about something you're reading, you usually
   a. read the section again.
   b. check in another book.
   c. discuss it with your teacher.
   d. hope that it isn't very important.

Rate Yourself

Discuss your answers with a partner. Decide together which response would work best for each situation. Then reread the choices you did not choose and explain why they are not the best course of action.

Questions for Clarity

In Lesson 16, you learned about the importance of being able to form mental pictures. In this activity, you will work with a partner to combine your skill in questioning with your ability to form clear mental pictures.

You and your partner will take turns describing a particular place. You might describe your room, a museum, a park, a festival, a farm, or a place you visited while on vacation. Once you have completed your description, your partner will ask you all the questions he or she needs to be able to create a clear mental picture of the place you have described. Then switch roles. Your partner will give a description, and you get to ask the questions.

Finally, discuss these questions about the questions you asked each other.

◆ Did you ask many questions that required simple *yes* or *no* answers?

◆ Did you ask open-ended questions, ones that required longer answers?

◆ Did you have to rephrase any questions?

◆ How did your questions help you create better mental pictures?

Use Your Curiosity

Most people don't read every word in a newspaper. They use the headlines to decide which stories to read. If the headline gives you all the information you need, you may not need to read the whole article. But if the headline raises more questions in your mind, you'll probably read on to answer your questions. A headline like *Home team loses on fumble* may tell a casual sports fan everything he or she wants to know: Our team lost. For other readers, the headline may raise questions such as these: Who made the fumble? Was it a close, exciting game? What did the coach have to say about it? What did the player who fumbled have to say? For these readers, their questions have aroused their curiosity.

Read each newspaper headline. Make up a question for each headline. Then draw a star beside the headline whose story you'd most like to read.

1. Cause of Air Crash Found

_____

_____

2. Vegetables Can Be Bad for You

_____

_____

3. Teen Drug Use Is Down

_____

_____

4. New Safety Device Prevents Car Accidents

_____

_____

5. Cure Found for Deadly Disease

_____

_____

Asking and Answering Questions

Tips for Better Questions and Answers

◆ Choose an appropriate time to ask your question. Does the speaker encourage questions during the presentation? Should you save your questions until the end?

◆ If you must save your question until the end of the presentation, jot it down. If the question is answered later in the speech, cross out the question and make a note of the answer.

◆ Think before you speak. Use simple, straightforward language.

◆ Set the stage. Tie in your question with something the speaker said. You may want to begin with: *You told us that . . . ,* or *Does this mean . . . ?*

◆ Listen carefully to the answer. If the answer raises a new question in your mind, ask that question, too.

◆ If the speaker doesn't understand your question or doesn't give the answer you need, rephrase your question.

◆ Be polite and courteous. Don't interrupt while the speaker is answering your question.

◆ Don't be afraid of appearing foolish. If you have a question, someone else probably has the same question. Other listeners will be glad you asked.

◆ Don't get so involved with your own question that you forget to listen to the questions of others. The answers to their questions will help you, too.

Conquering Your Fears

Many students are timid when it comes to asking and answering questions in class. Often, they feel intimidated for fear of asking a question that others might ridicule. Does this sometimes happen to you?

If it does, don't feel bad. It is a fear you can overcome. Start slowly by answering your teacher's questions when you're sure you know the answer. Get used to hearing yourself speak confidently. Gradually start asking your own questions. Soon you'll find you enjoy being a more active, involved member of the class!

Get Involved

Asking and answering questions during class does a lot more for you than simply clarifying things you don't understand. It also transforms you into an active listener and a more attentive student. If you're paying close enough attention to realize that there are things you don't understand, you're apt to be more focused and alert. And that means you're getting the most out of the time you spend in class.

Question Yourself

When you're reading, create your own questions by turning chapter heads and subheads into questions using the words *Who, What, When, Where, Why,* and *How.* By making up your own questions, you've set your own goals and purposes for reading. You've given yourself a reason to dig in and read.

But what happens if you can't answer your questions when you're working independently? Jot your questions down or mark them with sticky notes. Later you can discuss your questions with your teacher or a study partner.

The Best Time to Ask

Here's a project you can try with some classmates to find the best system for asking and answering questions. Form a small group and assign one person to be the speaker. Find a textbook or a class handout to use. Then try three different questioning strategies. The speaker should read a different textbook selection each time. Each selection should be two or three paragraphs long. Follow these steps:

1. For the first trial, listeners will simply call out any questions that come to mind as the speaker reads.

2. For the second trial, ask the listeners to raise their hands when they have a question. The speaker must acknowledge raised hands as soon as he or she comes to a good stopping point.

3. For the third trial, tell listeners to jot down their questions on a piece of paper and ask them when the speaker is done reading.

When you're finished, discuss as a group which system seemed to work the best. Name different situations in which each method might work best.

Where Are You Going?

Summarize what you learned in this lesson. _____

_____

_____

_____

Now use your summary to write a ***Take Charge!*** goal that will help you become a better student.

_____

_____

_____

_____

Making Your Vocabulary Grow

Words, Words, Words!

Dear Wordsmith,

I love words! Words, words, words! I know a lot of words now, but I want to know more. I learn new words in school every day, but even that's not enough. I just can't stop! I want to learn them on my own, but I don't know how. Can you help me?

Word Wonk

Dear Word Wonk,

Good for you! Your hunger for words is a problem more people should have. The more words you know, the more you can learn. And the more you learn, the more words you know. And that's good. The simplest and best advice I can offer is this: Read, read, read! That's the best way to learn new words. And you'll find other interesting ways to learn new words in your next *Take Charge!* lesson. Stay word hungry.

Wordsmith

Where Do You Stand?

How word hungry are you? Do you take time to improve your vocabulary? There are many simple ways to increase your word knowledge each and every day. Answer the questions below. Study your answers to plan new ways to make your vocabulary grow.

1. How many books do you read each month? (Don't include schoolbooks.) _____

2. Do you spend more time reading or watching television? _____

3. Do you ask your teacher questions when he or she uses a word you are not familiar with?

   _____

4. Do you jot down new words you hear and look them up in the dictionary later?

   _____

5. When you write a story or report for school do you revise your first draft to try to use more descriptive words?

   _____

6. How often do you do crossword puzzles or other word games in your spare time?

   _____

Have Fun With Words

Get together with a partner and make word puzzles for each other. Use a vocabulary list from one of your classes, or make up your own list of words you need to know for an upcoming test.

Before you begin, learn about different kinds of word puzzles you can make. Choose one type of puzzle to make for your partner in the space below. Then exchange puzzles and figure them out.

1. **rebus:** a pictorial representation of a word

   – ppy + zz +  – af = <u>puzzle</u>

2. **word search:** words hidden among letters

   f u z p u z z l e h i

3. **crossword:** an arrangement of numbered squares filled with words running across and down

   | P | u | z | z | l | e |

   e

   u

   s

4. **anagram:** a word or phrase formed by reordering the letters of another word or phrase   dirty room = dormitory

5. **palindrome:** a word or phrase that reads the same backwards or forwards

   Step on no pets.

W O R D   P U Z Z L E

Make Your Vocabulary GROW!

Build Your Word Collection

Collecting words from the world around you can be a hobby like collecting shells on a beach. Your vocabulary collection will be unique. You can share and trade words with other word lovers. The best way to make your word collection grow is to read everything you can get your hands on, from cereal boxes to encyclopedias. You can also collect words you learn in class, words you hear in conversations, and words you hear or see on television.

Write your new words on note cards. Put a rubber band around the cards or place them in a file box or large envelope. Organize your words in alphabetical order. Each time you add new words to your collection, review all the words. Try to use one or two of your words each day.

Use Context Clues

You probably won't need to look up every new word you come across. Often you can use context clues to figure out the meaning of an unfamiliar word. Writers in different subject areas tend to provide different kinds of context clues to help you figure out new words. In science, you might find complete definitions of new words built right into the text. Look at this example:

> *The ecosystem, a specific situation in which a group of living organisms interact with their environment, is the basic unit of ecology.*

It shouldn't be too tough for you to figure out what an *ecosystem* is.

In social studies, writers may provide synonyms to help, like this:

> *The fibers were spun into yarn, then tied into hanks, or coils, and set aside to be woven.*

As you can see, a *hank* is a coil. The more practice you get using context to discover word meanings, the easier it will become.

Recognize Word Structure

Study prefixes, suffixes, and roots. You can often figure out the meanings of new words by breaking them down into parts. Look at the word *geology*. If you know that the root *geo* has something to do with the earth, and that the suffix *logy* means "study of," then you can guess that *geology* means "the study of the earth." If you look up the word *geology* in a dictionary, here's what you'll find: "The scientific study of the origin, history, and structure of the earth." That's pretty close!

Don't Count the Dictionary Out

Even though context clues can often help you understand unfamiliar words, vocabulary reference books are still important tools. Make the dictionary and thesaurus your best friends. Know how to use them and what kinds of information they include. Keep these books at your side as you read, and don't be shy about interrupting your reading to look up a word if you don't understand it from context. Reading on when you don't understand a word is a real waste of time.

Many dictionaries and encyclopedias are available on CD-ROM.

Do-It-Yourself Vocabulary List

Here's a long-term project that can help your vocabulary grow every single day! Create a word-a-day vocabulary calendar. You can use blank calendar pages. Or you can make a list of dates with space to write a word, its pronunciation, and its definition beside each one.

You can search for interesting words by looking through a dictionary or thesaurus. But the easiest way to find words for your calendar is just to keep your eyes and ears open. Whenever you read or hear an interesting but unfamiliar word, write it in the next open date in your calendar. Then look up the word to find its correct pronunciation and definition.

Check your calendar every morning. Say the word and its definition three times. Make a game of trying to sneak the word into your conversation or writing at least three times during the day. Once a week, review the new words you've learned.

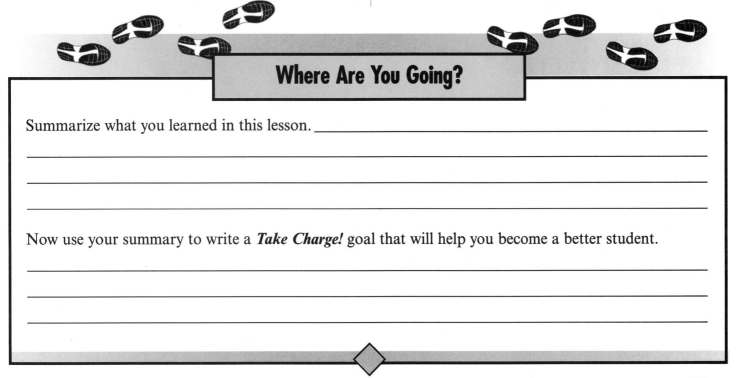

Where Are You Going?

Summarize what you learned in this lesson. _____

_____

_____

_____

Now use your summary to write a *Take Charge!* goal that will help you become a better student.

_____

_____

_____

Taking Paraphrased Notes

> Thebasiclawsofidealfrictionless fluidsweregivenmathematicalformbyLeo nhardEulerin1755.Eulerbasedhisworkinpa rtonearlierworkbyDanielandJacquesBer noulli.In1827,ClaudeNavierderivedtheequ ationsofviscousflow,whichwerepublished bySirGeorgeGabrielStokesin1845. . .

In Other Words . . .

Did you know that it's possible to hear more than 7,000 words in one hour of class time? That's a lot of words to hear, understand, and remember! Would you want—or be able—to write down every word while taking notes?

And think about all the words in all the books you are assigned to read. Did you know that an entire chapter of a book can be condensed into a page or two of notes? How can you do that? Easily! It's called *paraphrasing*.

Where Do You Stand?

Try this experiment. Find a couple of medium-sized paragraphs from one of your textbooks. On a separate sheet of paper, copy the paragraphs word-for-word, using a watch with a second hand to time yourself as you write. Then, time yourself as you take notes on the paragraphs again. This time, just write the most important ideas in your own words.

When you've completed the experiment, answer these questions:

1. What was the difference in your times?

_____

2. How much of your fastest writing can you read? _____

_____

3. How much of what you copied word-for-word is necessary information?

_____

_____

4. What conclusions can you draw from the experiment?

_____

_____

Rate Yourself

Trying to take down every word isn't likely to work very well. The notes you took in your own words were probably quicker to write and easier to understand. Writing ideas in your own words is called *paraphrasing*.

Practice Oral Paraphrasing

With a partner, find out how good you are at listening and comprehending. Ask your partner to read a selection from a textbook or an encyclopedia. Sit and listen as your partner reads. Then use your own words to tell what has just been said. This might take a little practice! In time you'll get better at identifying and summing up the important ideas in what you have heard.

From oral paraphrasing, it's just a short step to paraphrasing as you take notes. Using a different selection, repeat the activity with your partner. This time, write paraphrased notes of what you hear on the lines below.

_____

_____

_____

_____

_____

_____

_____

_____

_____

_____

Familiar Ideas, Unfamiliar Words

Proverbs are familiar sayings. The proverbs below, however, have been rewritten to disguise them. Paraphrase these wordy versions by writing the familiar proverb on the lines below. Like all good paraphrasing, the familiar proverb is short and concise.

1. Superfluous chefs destroy the soup.

_____

2. A member of the avian species in the fist is of more value than two members of the avian species in a shrub.

_____

3. When the feline has departed, the rodents will cavort.

_____

4. Survey the area before you jump.

_____

5. You can't keep your angel food and devour it also.

_____

6. If you can't overcome them, participate with them.

_____

7. If the sandal is the correct size, put it on.

_____

8. You can't educate an elderly canine to perform unfamiliar stunts.

_____

_____

Tips for Paraphrasing

Paraphrasing When Listening

◆ Don't try to make a word-for-word record of everything said in class. No matter what form your notes take, or whose words you are listening to, write down only the most important ideas or the facts you think you need to remember.

◆ Try to capture the speaker's meaning in as few words as possible. Leave out little words like *a*, *an*, and *the*. Use the & sign and other abbreviations.

◆ Don't paraphrase when the speaker's words include terms you need to remember. Use the terms and make sure you know how to spell them correctly.

◆ Concentrate on the main ideas of the presentation rather than on specific details.

◆ If there's something you don't quite understand, you may not be able to paraphrase. In that case, write down the speaker's exact words and surround them with quotation marks. Write a large question mark in the margin so you can come back and review the idea later.

◆ Try to catch vivid or striking words and phrases that your teacher uses. Write them down and use quotation marks. They'll help you reconstruct the lesson when you are studying from your notes.

Wilma Rudolph

Paraphrasing From Research

Paraphrasing is also a good technique to use when you're doing research. As you do your research, write the ideas and facts you plan to use in your own words on index cards. Also note the source of the information.

Sometimes you'll want to use a direct quote to make a point. Anytime you copy words without paraphrasing, remember to use quotation marks. Then when you use the quote in your speech or report, explain that the words are a direct quote and give the name of the author.

Read the excerpt about Olympic star Wilma Rudolph below. Then read the sample note cards on the next page. They show how you might take notes by paraphrasing and quoting different parts of the article.

Olympic All-Stars
Wilma Rudolph, Track and Field, 1960

When Wilma Rudolph was born, no one expected her to grow up to be an athlete. In fact, no one expected her to survive. The seventeenth child in a family of nineteen, Wilma was a very tiny baby. She lived her first few years as an invalid. Wilma had contracted polio when she was four. Doctors predicted that Rudolph would never walk again, but Rudolph's parents refused to accept the doctors' predictions, and the whole family worked together to help with little Wilma's therapy.

Rudolph learned to walk with a leg brace and then a special shoe. She refused to let her physical problems stop her. She qualified for the 1956 Olympics in track and field while she was still in high school. In 1960, she again went to the Summer Games. This time, she became the first American woman to win three gold medals in track. For this accomplishment, the Associated Press voted her U.S. Female Athlete of the Year. However, Rudolph's greatest victory was not at the Olympics; her greatest victory was her triumph over illness.

Paraphrased Notes

This note card summarizes information from the article. The information is paraphrased.

Wilma Rudolph
- 17th of 19 children in family. Tiny baby, almost didn't survive.
- polio when she was 4 yrs. old, doctors said she'd never walk
- whole family worked to help her + she learned to walk again
- 1960 olympics - won 3 gold medals in track! (1st U.S. woman to do that)

Source: "Olympic All-Stars." Reading for Information. Columbus, OH: Zaner-Bloser, Inc., 1997, p. 93.

Direct Quotations

This note card records several direct quotations from the article. The words are placed in quotation marks.

Wilma Rudolph
"Rudolph learned to walk with a leg brace and then a special shoe. She refused to let her physical problems stop her."
"the Associated Press voted her U.S. Female Athlete of the Year."
"Rudolph's greatest victory was not at the Olympics; her greatest victory was her triumph over illness."

Source: "Olympic All-Stars." Reading for Information. Columbus, OH: Zaner-Bloser, Inc., 1997, p. 93.

Where Are You Going?

Summarize what you learned in this lesson. _____

_____

_____

_____

Now use your summary to write a *Take Charge!* goal that will help you become a better student.

_____

_____

_____

Study Strategies for Reading

All those letters and numbers stand for something, but what?

Letter Scramble

Keeshia is confused. She's heard of the study methods called SQ3R and PRQT. She's even used them both at one time or another. But they still keep getting all mixed up in her head. Keeshia knows they're supposed to be helpful, but she has trouble remembering how they work.

Special study plans like SQ3R and PRQT may seem to be extra work at first. But with practice they become habits. And once they do, they make studying seem as easy as learning the alphabet.

Where Do You Stand?

Do you already use parts of SQ3R and PRQT? Check the statements that describe your study habits.

☐ Before I read a chapter in my textbook, I look through the pages and read headings and picture captions.

☐ I write down questions about things I expect to learn.

☐ I read the chapter introduction and summary.

☐ If there are review questions in the chapter, I read them first.

☐ I read the chapter carefully.

☐ I say important ideas aloud.

☐ I review by looking back at the headings and pictures and thinking about the chapter's main ideas.

☐ I make up quizzes to test myself to see how much I learned from my reading.

Rate Yourself

How many statements did you check? Each activity is a part of one of the study methods SQ3R or PRQT. If you already do some of the steps, you're ahead of the game. All you need is a good review of these step-by-step study plans.

Review SQ3R

SQ3R is a system to help you remember what you read. The letters in SQ3R stand for **S**urvey, **Q**uestion, **R**ead, **R**ecite, and **R**eview. Jog your memory by reading the summary of each step.

With a partner, use the SQ3R study method with a section of one of your social studies, science, or other textbooks.

Survey—Before reading, look over the whole chapter to get the big picture. Read the title and introduction, headings and picture captions, and the conclusion.

Question—Prepare to be an active reader by asking yourself questions. Read the questions in the chapter or make up your own by adding *who, what, when, where, why,* and *how* to chapter heads and subheads.

Read—By the time you actually begin reading the chapter, you'll already know a lot about the material. Since the material is already familiar, you'll find that it's easier to remember.

Recite—Summarize what you've learned by saying it out loud to a partner, yourself, or the dog. Hearing the words helps you remember.

Review—Go back through the chapter, skimming headings, subheadings, and captions. Summarize main ideas and answer the questions you made up. You'll be surprised to see how much you know.

Review PRQT

PRQT works on the same principle as SQ3R. The steps are a little different, but you'll accomplish the same thing.

Again with your partner, use the PRQT method with a different section of one of your textbooks.

Preview is the same as surveying the chapter.

Read and **Q**uestion at the same time. Read each paragraph or section. Then make up a question about what you've read. Write the question on a note card with the page number and answer on the back.

Test yourself after you've completed your reading. Use the question-and-answer cards you made. Keep going through your cards until you can answer every question.

Compare Study Methods

Now meet with a small group of classmates to discuss the pros and cons of each study method.

After your discussion, decide which method works best for you. On the lines below, write the method you chose and your reasons for choosing it.

_____

_____

_____

_____

_____

_____

More Study Methods

Find the Right Study System

PRQT and SQ3R are time-tested study systems. Over the years, many people have tried them out and modified them for their own purposes.

Here are some other study methods you may want to try. They're similar, but each one is a little different. Try each method on your own to find the one that's comfortable for you. Think carefully! The study method you choose now may be the one you use for the rest of your life.

PRQST

PRQST is almost the same as PRQT. It simply adds a step that you may find helpful.

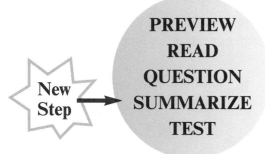

New Step →

**PREVIEW
READ
QUESTION
SUMMARIZE
TEST**

PREVIEW, READ, and QUESTION just as you would for PRQT. But as you read, stop at the end of each section to take notes that SUMMARIZE what you've read. Review your notes before you move on to the final step in which you TEST yourself. You may be surprised at how much this one extra step adds to the PRQT system!

PROTO

SQ3R, PRQT, and PRQST are all good methods for reading chapters in textbooks or articles in reference materials. PROTO is a study technique that works with novels, short stories, and essays as well as with textbooks and articles. Read the description of this study method below. You might find it works well for you!

- **P**review the material to get a grasp of the general idea. Pay careful attention to titles and headings.

- **R**ead the material, watching for main ideas and key points. Read and reread as many times as you need to. When you feel that you understand the material, go on to the next step.

- **O**rganize the information. Think about the way the information was presented and the best organizational strategy that you can use to recall the material. Choose from among strategies such as comparison and contrast, cause and effect, and sequence of events.

- **T**ake Notes based on the organizational strategy you've selected. Graphic organizers are a great way to organize your notes. You might make an outline, a web, or a chart. Whatever you choose, make sure to list key points and details under the appropriate main ideas.

- **O**verview your notes when they're finished. Review and summarize to make sure you've got the big picture. Then fill in the details by reviewing the facts.

Give me a P. Give me an R. Give me an O. Give me a T. Give me another O!

Make a K-W-L Chart

When using the K-W-L technique, start by making a chart like the one below. Before reading, brainstorm what you already KNOW about the subject. Write your ideas in the first column. Then think as specifically as you can about what you WANT to find out from your reading. Write your questions in the second column. When you've finished reading, fill in the LEARN column with the new things you've learned.

K-W-L is a process for studying. If you find out that any of the ideas in the KNOW column were incorrect, make a note of that, too. You may find that the new things you learn raise even more questions. If so, revise the second column of your chart.

What I KNOW	What I WANT to Know	What I LEARNED

Where Are You Going?

Summarize what you learned in this lesson. _____

_____

_____

_____

Now use your summary to write a *Take Charge!* goal that will help you become a better student.

_____

_____

_____

Taking Notes From Reading

Meet Teri

Teri has a problem. One night she stayed up late to do research for a report. As she grew tired, the notes she was taking changed. Instead of paraphrasing what she was reading, Teri started copying whole sentences right out of the book. She was so tired she didn't even notice what she was doing.

When the time came to write her report, she used the notes she had taken. Parts of Teri's report sounded familiar to her teacher, and he took the time to check it out. Now Teri's in trouble for using another writer's words, or *plagiarizing*. Following some simple note-taking rules would have saved Teri lots of worry and embarrassment.

Where Do You Stand?

Could you find yourself in Teri's shoes? Take this quiz to find out how well you understand the rules for note-taking. Write *True* or *False* before each statement.

1. _____ Plagiarizing is using another writer's words as your own.

2. _____ Plagiarizing refers only to copying from another classmate's paper.

3. _____ It's okay to use information you find in a book as long as you put it in your own words and identify the original source.

4. _____ It's okay to use another writer's words as long as you put them in quotation marks and tell who wrote them.

5. _____ One way to avoid accidental plagiarizing is to paraphrase, or put ideas into your own words, as you take notes.

6. _____ Plagiarizing won't cause you any trouble as long as you didn't mean to do it.

Rate Yourself

How did you do? If you answered *True* to questions 1, 3, 4, and 5 and *False* to questions 2 and 6, you probably have a good idea of the right ways to take notes. If not, this lesson will help you learn to avoid trouble and take good notes.

Practice Taking Notes

Read the article at the bottom of the page. On the lines in the next column, write a summary of what you read.

When you are finished, work with a partner to compare the summaries you wrote with the original article. Did either of you plagiarize, or copy whole parts of the text word-for-word? It's okay to use some words and phrases from the article. Just make sure you used your own words to explain the main ideas.

_____

_____

_____

_____

_____

_____

_____

_____

The Savanna Food Chain

Animals of the Savanna

No biome on Earth provides a more dramatic backdrop for the ceaseless struggle for survival in the animal kingdom than the tropical savannas of Africa. These vast arid oceans of tall, swaying grass teem with animal life. Insects, birds, and especially large hoofed herbivores, such as zebras, wildebeests, gazelles, elands, topis, and hartebeests, feast on the abundant vegetation, while carnivores —lions, cheetahs, leopards, and African wild dogs—crouch low in the grasses, waiting for the opportunity to pounce. Scavengers pace restlessly nearby or hover in the blue sky above, anxiously waiting to devour what remains when the carnivores have eaten their fill. The plants, herbivores, carnivores, and scavengers of the savanna provide an ideal example of an ecosystem in action.

The Food Chain

The term "food chain" is used to describe the way energy from the sun is transferred from one life form to another, changing form along the way. This is how the food chain of the savanna works: First, energy from the sun is collected by grasses and other plants, which use the sun's energy and the process of photosynthesis to manufacture sugars and starches. Next, the plants are eaten by herbivores, whose bodies become repositories for the nutritional components obtained from the plants. Herbivores, in turn, are devoured by carnivores, which, under normal conditions, take only the most nutritious parts of their prey. Whatever remains after the carnivores are finished is taken by scavengers. Nothing is wasted in the savanna food chain, because what is left by scavengers serves to fertilize the soil, which, in turn, nourishes new plant life.

Tips for Careful Note-Taking

Chunking will help you digest information a little bit at a time.

Copyrights and Wrongs

Have you ever noticed the copyright on a book? Usually it is located in the front of the book on the back side of the title page. Copyrights are a form of protection for writers and artists. It protects the works they create.

When a piece of writing is copyrighted, it means it is the property of the author, just like a bicycle or a television is the property of the person who owns it. No one else can publish that piece of writing without obtaining the permission of the author. If you use a writer's work word-for-word in your paper without quotation marks and without giving the author credit, you are stealing something that belongs to someone else. Almost everything you read or take notes from is copyrighted, so be careful!

A Dictionary Can Help

You're most likely to copy right out of the book when you don't understand an idea well enough to put it into your own words. Before you write any notes, make sure you understand the ideas. Look up unfamiliar words in the dictionary. If you're running short of time or don't have a dictionary handy, copy the words from the book and put them in quotation marks. Later, when you have more time and access to a dictionary, rewrite the words in quotation marks into your own words.

Scan and Chunk

Scan your assignment. Then read it in small chunks. Scanning will help you find out what you're supposed to know. Chunking will help you digest the information a little bit at a time. Taking notes about a chunk of information, instead of sentence by sentence, will help you keep from inadvertently copying ideas word-for-word.

3 x 5 = Power

Use the power of the 3 x 5 index card. These cards are especially useful when you are writing a report or doing a research paper. Create a source card for every source of information you use, whether it's a book, a newspaper or magazine article, an interview, an audiotape, or any other research material.

Then take your notes, writing only one piece of information on each card. Record the source of the information on the card. Then sort your cards to construct an outline for your paper. If you're using more than one source, make sure ideas from different sources are mixed together.

Turn back to page 79. The illustration shows note cards—one with paraphrased information and one that quotes directly from the source. You can use these cards as a model when you make your own.

Note-Taking DOs and DON'Ts

DOs

Do paraphrase what you read by putting your notes into your own words.

Do summarize information instead of trying to note every detail.

Do take your notes on 3 x 5 index cards and cite the source of the information on each card.

Do use a dictionary or thesaurus to help you understand the author's ideas and find different ways to say them.

Do use quotation marks whenever you want to remember the exact words of the writer. If you use those words in your writing, be sure to tell your reader the source.

DON'Ts

Don't copy word-for-word from a book unless you have a special reason for doing so.

Don't write your notes in whole sentences. Instead, write key words and phrases.

Don't quote another writer without giving him or her credit for the writing.

Don't try to take notes when you're too tired. When you're tired, you're more likely to take the easy way out by copying from the book, and you may not even realize that you're doing it.

Where Are You Going?

Summarize what you learned in this lesson. _____

_____

_____

_____

Now use your summary to write a **_Take Charge!_** goal that will help you become a better student.

_____

_____

_____

Monitoring Comprehension

Give Yourself Feedback

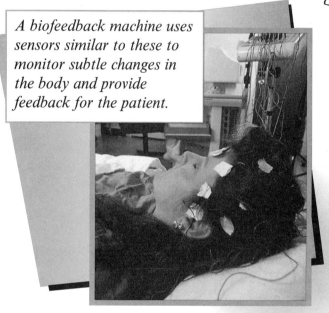

A biofeedback machine uses sensors similar to these to monitor subtle changes in the body and provide feedback for the patient.

Have you ever heard of *biofeedback*? Biofeedback is a medical technique that uses special equipment to monitor bodily functions like heart rate or blood pressure. The theory behind biofeedback is that by constantly monitoring, or being aware of, what is going on inside his or her own body, a patient can learn to take control. Biofeedback techniques have been found to be effective in treating conditions like high blood pressure and migraine headaches.

Monitoring your comprehension as you read is a lot like biofeedback. By making yourself aware of your reading comprehension, you take control of your own learning.

Where Do You Stand?

You don't need a fancy machine to monitor your reading comprehension. You just need to train your mind to focus on the right things. See how aware you were as you read the lesson introduction by answering these questions.

1. Were you feeling calm or nervous as you read the introduction? _____

_____

2. Was your body tense or relaxed?

_____

3. Did you focus your attention on what you were reading? _____

_____

4. Describe all the sounds you could hear as you read. _____

_____

5. Describe the stray thoughts that went through your head while you were reading. _____

_____

_____

6. Without rereading the first paragraph, define *biofeedback*. _____

_____

_____

Rate Yourself

How did you do? Were you aware of the feelings you had while you read? Did noises and stray thoughts distract you?

Unfortunately, unlike biofeedback, there is no special equipment to monitor your focus and comprehension. But there are strategies that you can learn and use, strategies that will help you improve your comprehension skills. Read on to find out more.

Be Aware

Find a partner to be your biofeedback machine. Tell your partner to stop you at random intervals while you read a textbook selection. Each time your partner stops you, write a brief summary of what you've just read on the lines below. If your mind was wandering while you read, write down what you were thinking about instead. If you were aware that you weren't concentrating on your reading, make a star beside your description.

1. _____
   _____
   _____

2. _____
   _____
   _____

3. _____
   _____
   _____

4. _____
   _____
   _____

Keep Your Focus

Here's your chance to break some rules and see what happens. Select a textbook chapter you haven't read yet. Then ask a partner to try to distract you as you read. Your partner may hum, talk, tap pencils, or do anything that is not so loud that it distracts the rest of the class. Your partner may not touch you. When you finish reading, answer the questions.

1. What was the main idea of what you read?
   _____
   _____

2. Name three details you recall. _____
   _____
   _____

3. Write three things you read in order. _____
   _____
   _____

4. What was the most distracting thing your partner did? _____
   _____
   _____

5. What techniques helped you maintain your concentration? _____
   _____
   _____

Tips for Monitoring Comprehension as You Read

Learn to Shift Gears

Attentive drivers constantly shift their eyes from the road ahead to the rearview mirror. Even though their main goal is to stay on the road and out of the way of other cars, they need to be aware of what's going on around them at all times.

Monitoring comprehension works the same way. The best way to make sure you're understanding what you read is to take frequent glances at your mental rearview mirror. This means you check your comprehension at the end of every chapter, every section, or even every paragraph if the material is difficult. Each time you glance into that mental mirror, ask yourself these questions:

◆ Can I put the ideas into my own words?

◆ Do I need to look up any vocabulary words?

◆ Do I understand how the new information fits in with information I've learned before?

◆ Should I read some sections over again?

◆ Can I predict what will happen next?

If there are some things you didn't fully understand, go back and reread. If there are words you don't know, look them up. Make a prediction about what's coming next, then read on to see if your prediction was correct.

When You Just Can't Concentrate . . .

Monitoring your comprehension is the key to knowing when you're wasting time by just letting your eyes flow over the page without engaging your mind. Often just realizing that your mind is wandering can be enough to bring your attention back to the page. When it's not, try these tips.

◆ **Take a short break.** Maybe your mind is just too tired or overloaded with facts to keep going. If you're at home, get up and walk to another room or get a healthy snack. If you're at school, stretch at your seat, look around the room, and then get back to work.

◆ **Switch subjects.** If you don't have time for a break, give yourself a change of pace instead. Stop reading and do some math problems or write that poem for English class. When your mind feels more relaxed, you can get back to your reading.

◆ **Change your environment.** If you're at home, get up and move to another room. Move from a soft chair to a hard one. Turn off the radio or television. If you're at school, changing your environment will be harder. But you can do it by refocusing your attention, blocking out the distractions, and imagining yourself in another place.

◆ **Check for mental blocks.** Is a bad feeling holding you back? Maybe you got a bad grade on your last quiz, so you're nervous about the next one. Maybe you don't like the subject, the teacher, or even the person who sits beside you in class, so you don't like to go there. Figure out what's causing your mental block. Once you do that, it's likely to go away.

Monitor Information Flow

Monitor the way information flows through your mind as you work. Monitoring information flow means taking what you've read and moving it through different parts of your brain to make it a permanent part of your personal data bank. Methods for monitoring information flow include:

◆ Summarizing the information in your mind

◆ Saying it out loud to yourself in your own words

◆ Writing it down

◆ Explaining it to another person

Write It Down

Writing information down is important for two reasons. The obvious reason is that, by taking notes or making an outline, you will have something permanent to refer to in case you forget what you've read. The more important reason, though, is that writing information down is the most effective way of processing new information. Just the act of writing it out will help transfer the new information from your short-term to your long-term memory. And that's the secret to turning information from a book into personal knowledge.

Explaining what you have read to another person is a great way to monitor the information you are learning.

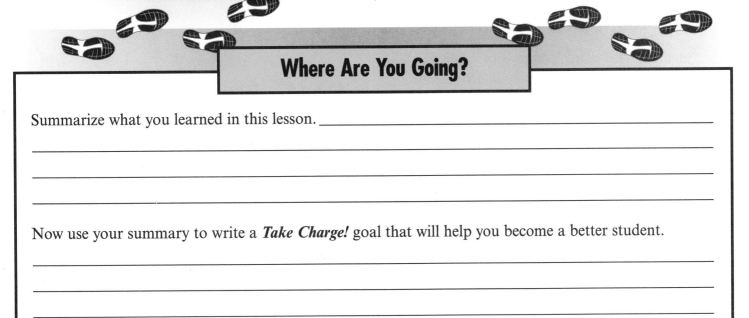

Where Are You Going?

Summarize what you learned in this lesson. _____

_____

_____

_____

Now use your summary to write a ***Take Charge!*** goal that will help you become a better student.

_____

_____

_____

LESSON 23

Revising Notes

I hear and I forget.
I see and I remember.
I do and I understand.
— Chinese Proverb

Tell me and I'll forget.
Show me and I may not remember.
Involve me, and I'll understand.
— Native American Saying

Get Involved in Your Reading

One way to get involved in your reading is to read actively. And one way to read actively is to take notes. Deciding which notes to take makes you think about the ideas in your book. The act of writing them down helps you remember them.

Taking notes is the first step toward remembering what you read. Using your notes to study is another step. But what if you find that the notes you took quickly while you had the book in front of you are almost impossible to read when you need them? Don't worry. Revising your notes will bring everything back.

Where Do You Stand?

There are many good methods for revising notes. Some work better than others for different people, and some work best with different subjects. How many of these methods are familiar to you? Check the methods you are familiar with and the methods you use regularly.

Method	I know how to do this.	I use this method regularly.
Recopying		
Highlighting or color-coding		
Drawing webs		
Making outlines		
Organizing ideas on note cards		
Designing study sheets		

Rate Yourself

If you're familiar with a variety of ways to revise notes, you're ahead of the game. If you regularly use different techniques, that's even better. It's a good idea to try different ways to revise notes. Then you can choose the methods that work best for you.

Sort It Out

In the next column, you'll find some notes taken by Kevin several weeks ago. With a little bit of revising, they'll be much more useful to Kevin. Read through the notes. Identify the main ideas and key details. Then organize and revise the notes in the space below by placing the information in a web or in an outline. If you really want to practice revising notes, make both a web and an outline!

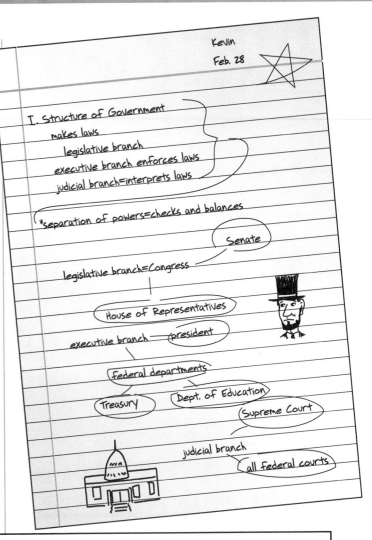

Methods for Revising Notes

Recopy Your Notes

Recopying your notes is an easy way to revise. When you recopy, you just rewrite your notes in your neatest handwriting, checking the spelling of key names and terms, and filling in any information that is unclear. When you recopy your notes, they are still organized in the same way, but they are easier to read and understand.

Recopying is easy, and it helps you remember. When you recopy, you have to look at your notes more carefully than you would if you just reread them. It also helps the information get to your brain through a different path—your sense of touch. If you read aloud as you recopy, you'll also be using your sense of hearing.

Highlight or Color Code

To make your recopied notes even more useful, you can go back and highlight, or color code, them. Make up a system that works well for the subject you're studying. In math, you might highlight formulas or definitions. For social studies, you might use one color for main ideas, another color for supporting details, and another color for names you want to remember. You can make your notes as colorful and creative as you please!

Design Graphic Organizers

You know that graphic organizers are good ways to organize information. If you think in pictures, using this method may help you see how ideas and facts are related. Plan your web ahead of time or just start writing ideas and see how it grows. The more personal you make your design, the easier it will be for you to remember the information. Here are two examples.

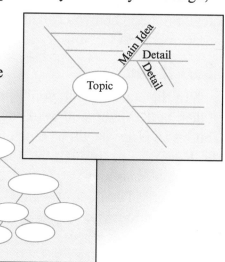

Make an Outline

An outline can make the organization of ideas very clear. It has a formal structure, with Roman numerals for main ideas and letters and numbers that show the relative importance of details. If you're an orderly person who likes everything to fit into just the right place, you may prefer making outlines to drawing maps or webs. Both methods help you organize information and show the relationships among ideas and details.

Organize With Note Cards

If you're a person who likes to work with your hands, using note cards to revise your notes may be just the thing for you. Once your notes have been copied onto the cards, you can move them around and use them in many ways. You can lay them out on your desk in the shape of a web. You can organize them like an outline. You can use them to quiz yourself to study for a test. And note cards are really portable. Put a rubber band around them and stick them in your pocket. Take them out to study while you're waiting in a long line or whenever you have a few minutes left at the end of a class.

Turn Your Notes Into Study Sheets

A study sheet is the final version of the raw notes that you have written and revised. It may include an outline, several graphic organizers, and complete paragraphs of information written in your own words. Once you've finalized your study sheets, put them all together in a three-ring binder. Use tabbed dividers to separate subjects.

When it's time for a test, you'll be able to use your study sheets to study better and faster. You'll know that you've got all the information you need in an organized, easy-to-read form. And once you feel organized, the rest is easy.

Take time to revise your "raw" notes into useful study aids.

Where Are You Going?

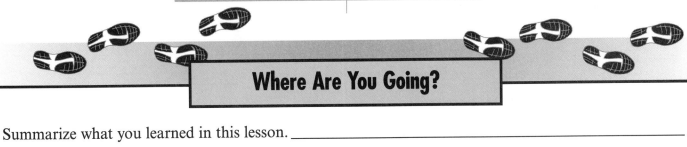

Summarize what you learned in this lesson. _____

_____

_____

_____

Now use your summary to write a ***Take Charge!*** goal that will help you become a better student.

_____

_____

_____

Selecting a Persuasive Topic

What Do You Care About?

Air Pollution Reaches Record High

Researchers Claim Link Between Nuclear Plant and Leukemia

Female Executives Still Earn 20% Less

The Last Tigers on the Planet?

What issues do you feel strongly about?

Issues are hot topics that have more than one side. People usually have strong feelings about issues, and they're usually ready to debate the issues, or present arguments for either side. Issues can be global, like preservation of rain forests, or local, like school dress codes.

If you feel strongly about an issue, chances are that you'd like to convince others to feel the same way. The only way to do that is to present a clear, logical case for your side.

Where Do You Stand?

There are many issues to think about. Some are global issues that affect people or other living things in different parts of the U.S. or the world. Some are local issues that are important to people in your town, your neighborhood, or even your school. What issues do you care about most? On the lines below, write five local issues and five global issues that concern you.

Local Issues

1. _____
2. _____
3. _____
4. _____
5. _____

Global Issues

1. _____
2. _____
3. _____
4. _____
5. _____

Narrow Your Topic

The Problem: Mrs. Munoz gave this assignment: Give a report that will persuade people to do something worthwhile. Ramon, Gita, and Ellie thought this was a great idea. They formed a group and chose the topic *saving endangered species*.

But things started to go wrong almost right away. One group member complained that they couldn't really solve such a big problem. The others were afraid they could never even make a dent in reading all the background material that was available. What could they do?

The Solution: The group sat down to discuss the problem. As they talked, Ramon, Gita, and Ellie realized that their topic was too broad. They decided to make it narrower and closer to home. After they decided on the topic *how to make the local pond a good habitat for wild animals*, their report went smoothly.

Your Turn: Your topic can make or break your project. Too broad a topic can be overwhelming. Too narrow a topic can leave you with nothing to say. Practice narrowing topics. For each broad topic below, write two narrow topics you could use for a report.

1. School rules

    a. _____

    b. _____

2. Pollution

    a. _____

    b. _____

3. Smoking

    a. _____

    b. _____

Organize Your Arguments

Discuss the topics you wrote with a partner. Then choose one topic and organize your ideas for a persuasive speech. Begin with a statement that tells how you feel about the issue. Then write three *pros,* or arguments that support your opinion, and three *cons,* or arguments against your opinion.

Statement _____

_____

_____

Pros	Cons
a. _____	**a.** _____
_____	_____
_____	_____
_____	_____
b. _____	**b.** _____
_____	_____
_____	_____
_____	_____
c. _____	**c.** _____
_____	_____
_____	_____
_____	_____

Tips for Choosing Your Best Topic

Grade Your Topic

Every time you choose a topic, fill in this report card. Answer *Yes* or *No* to each question. Your topic doesn't pass unless it earns a *Yes* answer to every question. Revise your topic and revise it again until it passes.

Topic Report Card

Topic: _____

_____

—— I can cover the topic adequately in the time I have.

—— I care enough about the topic to give an interesting presentation.

—— I can think of three or four good arguments to back up my opinion.

—— I will be able to find plenty of reference materials about the topic.

—— I can find at least two supporting details to prove each of my arguments.

Plan Your Presentation

Before you choose your final topic, think about how you plan to present your speech, project, or report. The kind of research you do will depend on the form your presentation will take. Think about how much your audience already knows about your topic and how much background information you'll need to give. Then decide on the best way to share your ideas. You may want to:

◆ Make a classroom display.

◆ Present a demonstration.

◆ Make a video.

◆ Present a slide show.

◆ Write a book and make an oral report about it.

◆ Make a tape recording.

◆ Write a play and perform it for the class.

◆ Make an oral report with posters and wall charts as visual aids.

The kind of presentation you plan will let you know whether or not you need to look for things like pictures, charts, or quotes as you do your research.

Plan Your Research

Before you finalize your topic, take a trip to the library to make sure the material you need is really there. Check general reference materials, like encyclopedias, for a brief overview of your topic. Check the card catalog and magazine indexes. Go on the Internet if you can. Consider using resources like these:

◆ Books, magazines, and newspapers

◆ People to interview

◆ An experiment, survey, or observation of your own

◆ Organizations to write to

◆ Videos and cassettes

◆ CD-ROMs or Web sites

Don't overlook interviewing an expert on your topic. Many people will be happy to share their knowledge and experience with you.

Your Project Notebook—Your Most Important Resource

As soon as a project is assigned, start a project notebook or set aside a special section for your project in your school notebook. Your project notebook will improve your organization by giving you a special place to record all the information you find. Begin by writing down possible topics. As you choose and narrow your topic, add important ideas that support your opinion. When you check the library for possible research materials, record the names and locations of sources that look interesting. You can come back to them later, when it's time to begin your research. A project notebook will help you save time and avoid stress. You'll always have all the information you need right at hand.

Here are some sections you might have in your project notebook:

◆ Topics
◆ Key Words
◆ Research Questions
◆ References and Other Sources
◆ Experiments and Observations
◆ Bibliography

Where Are You Going?

Summarize what you learned in this lesson. _____
_____
_____
_____

Now use your summary to write a *Take Charge!* goal that will help you become a better student.
_____
_____
_____

LESSON 25

Collecting and Organizing Information

Zach is collecting information for a report on river pollution. He's using the Internet as a resource.

Information, Please!

Once you've chosen a topic for a speech, report, or project, the next step is to collect and organize information. Brainstorming key words and ideas, making outlines, and taking notes are handy skills that will help you with this next important step. Whether you use encyclopedias for general background information, magazine articles, books, or the Internet, it's important to plan ahead and schedule plenty of time to research your topic thoroughly.

Where Do You Stand?

What is your style when it comes to researching and taking notes? Answer these questions to find out.

1. What method of note-taking do you use? Do you write notes on index cards or a note pad, or do you use another system?

_____

_____

2. What does it mean to "skim" an article? Do you use this skill when researching?

_____

_____

3. Do you write an outline before you begin writing a paper? Why or why not?

_____

_____

4. What's the best way to make sure you're not still doing research the day before the paper or speech is due?

_____

_____

Organize Your Thoughts

One way to start collecting information for your paper or speech is to brainstorm all the words that come to mind when you think of your topic. To help organize your ideas, use a web like this one on the topic of river pollution.

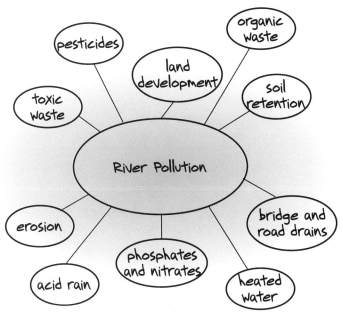

With a partner, choose a topic that interests both of you. If you wish, you can use the persuasive topic you selected in Lesson 24. Brainstorm key words about your topic and write them in a web in the space below.

Plan Your Research

What materials and resources can you use to prepare a speech or report? There are many sources of information available to you. Here are some suggestions to get you started.

◆ Your school or local library is a logical place to start. Look for books and periodicals that relate to your topic.

◆ Check your computer sources, including Web sites and CD-ROMs, for information on your topic.

◆ There may be experts on your topic in your community. You might contact and interview people at local universities, museums, businesses, government agencies, and even clubs who have an interest in your topic.

With your partner, think about the topic in your web. Then make a list of all the sources you might check for information on this topic.

Tips for Collecting and Organizing Information

1 Plan Your Time

When is your project due? How many days does that give you to complete your paper or speech? Work backward from the due date and make a calendar. Schedule time to gather information, make an outline, write a first draft, and so on. Keep to-do lists for every task on your schedule to help you keep track of your progress. Your project notebook will also help you organize your time efficiently (see page 99).

2 Make a General Outline

Review your web of key words and ideas about your topic, and then make a short, general outline of your paper or speech. This outline will show the order in which you plan to discuss your ideas. Your outline will help guide your research. You can, however, revise your outline as you learn more about your topic.

3 Skim and Scan

When you consult a reference book or a nonfiction information book, look for your topic in the index, located at the back of most books. For encyclopedias, look at the alphabetical listing or the separate index volume.

Skim the pages about your topic. Look for your key words in titles, subheadings, highlighted words and phrases, illustrations, and captions. If you find words related to your topic, scan the text under those headings or highlighted phrases. Take notes of relevant information on index cards.

4 Take Notes

◆ Use index cards to record information for your paper or speech. Put one idea or piece of information on each card. At the top of the card identify the topic with a short "headline." Then summarize the important information in your own words. If you use any direct quotations, put them in quotation marks. See page 79 for sample note cards.

◆ Look at your general outline. Decide where the information on your index card fits. Jot the appropriate outline letter and/or number in the upper right-hand corner of your card. If you're not sure where the information fits, use an asterisk (*) instead of a letter.

◆ At the bottom of the card, identify the source and page number. You can just use the author's last name.

◆ Make separate source cards listing the complete bibliographic information on each resource you use. For books record the title, author, publisher, and publication date and place. For magazines, you'll need the title, author, and page numbers of the article, and the magazine name, date, and volume number.

Organize Your Notes

After you've finished taking notes, review your outline and make changes based on your research. Then look at your note cards. Group together all the cards that share the same outline letter or number that you wrote in the right-hand corner of each card.

Within each topic group, sort the cards further. Put together all of the cards that share the same "headline."

Then read through your note cards, beginning at the front of the stack and reading to the back. Does the order make sense? Rearrange the cards until they're in a logical order. Be sure to review cards marked with an asterisk to figure out where they fit. Remember that you don't have to include all your cards; deciding what to leave out can be as important as deciding what to include.

Prepare a Bibliography

A *bibliography* is an alphabetical list of sources used for a paper or speech. It's usually found on the last page of a report.

Bibliography entries are written in a specific format. The teacher who assigns the paper may tell you what format to use. If not, use the formats below for books and magazine articles.

Book

Haslam, S.M. <u>River Pollution: An Ecological Perspective</u>. New York: John Wiley & Sons, 1994.

Magazine Article

Williams, Ted. "Reconnecting with Rivers." <u>Audubon</u>. Vol. 100, May-June 1998: 42–49.

Write a bibliography entry for a book called *Healthy Foods* by Dr. I.M. Hungry. The book was published in 1998 by Good Food Press, located in Breadbasket, Iowa.

_____

_____

_____

Where Are You Going?

Summarize what you learned in this lesson. _____

_____

_____

_____

Now use your summary to write a *Take Charge!* goal that will help you become a better student.

_____

_____

_____

Preparing for a Presentation

Is this how the audience looks to you when you make a speech?

The Three Ps

It's natural to be nervous about speaking in front of your classmates. But you won't feel as nervous if you are well prepared and confident. The best strategy for giving a great presentation is to follow the "Three Ps":

Prepare
◆ Decide on your main points.
◆ Make an outline.
◆ Write note cards ahead of time.

Practice
◆ Practice repeatedly in front of a mirror.
◆ Have a dress rehearsal in front of an audience.

Present
◆ Stand straight.
◆ Take deep breaths to relax.
◆ Speak slowly and clearly.

Where Do You Stand?

How confident do you feel about your speaking ability? Think about how you prepare for a presentation. Then read each statement. Circle the number on the scale that tells how often you do each of these.

1. I write main ideas and key words on note cards.

| Hardly Ever | ① | ② | ③ | ④ | ⑤ | Almost Always |

2. I avoid looking down and reading my whole speech.

| Hardly Ever | ① | ② | ③ | ④ | ⑤ | Almost Always |

3. I practice my speech at least five times before my final presentation.

| Hardly Ever | ① | ② | ③ | ④ | ⑤ | Almost Always |

4. I start my speech with an interesting quote, surprising statistic, or other hook to grab the audience's attention.

| Hardly Ever | ① | ② | ③ | ④ | ⑤ | Almost Always |

5. I speak slowly and clearly, and I make eye contact with my listeners.

| Hardly Ever | ① | ② | ③ | ④ | ⑤ | Almost Always |

Rate Yourself

To rate your presentation skills, add up the numbers you circled. Write your total in the box.

◆ If you scored over 20, you're probably a relaxed speaker. Learning new presentation techniques will make you a standout.

◆ If you scored between 12 and 19, the tips in this lesson will help you polish your presentations.

◆ If you scored between 5 and 11, you probably don't enjoy public speaking. Don't worry! The techniques in this lesson will help you feel less nervous and more confident.

What Do You Mean?

When you make a speech, you can use your voice to emphasize important points. The way you say a sentence can change its meaning. With a partner, practice saying the following sentence in different ways. Stress the underlined word each time. Then discuss the way your emphasis changed the meaning each time.

> **1.** <u>I</u> did not tell you to go there.
> **2.** I did <u>not</u> tell you to go there.
> **3.** I did not tell <u>you</u> to go there.
> **4.** I did not tell you to <u>go</u> there.
> **5.** I did not tell you to go <u>there</u>.

Evaluate the Speaker

Observe a speech given by a friend, a teacher, a local politician, or a speaker on television. With a partner, analyze the speech by answering the following questions:

1. How did the introduction grab your attention?

_____

_____

2. During what part of the speech did the speaker let you know what the main points would be?

_____

_____

3. What cues did the speaker use to let you know when a new topic or point was about to come up?

_____

_____

4. Did the conclusion include a summary of the speaker's main points? What were they?

_____

_____

5. How did the speaker use his or her voice for emphasis?

_____

_____

6. What gestures and movements did the speaker use?

_____

_____

Remember the Three Ps!

1 Prepare

Once you've written your outline, you'll need to remember what you plan to say. To do this, write index cards for each section of your presentation. Don't write your entire speech on the cards. Instead, write a topic sentence for each section. You might even write your first and last sentences word-for-word. Then write key words to remind you of your main points. If you have graphic aids, note when you plan to show them and what you'll say about each one.

2 Practice

- Practice your speech at least five times before you present it.

- Practice in front of a mirror, videotape yourself, or tape record your speech.

- Critique your own performance after each practice. Ask yourself questions like these:

    Was my introduction interesting?

    Did my gestures add emphasis, or were they distracting?

    Did I show my graphic aids so everyone could see them?

    Did my speech last an appropriate length of time?

- Have a "dress rehearsal" by presenting your speech for your family or a few friends.

- If you're doing a demonstration as part of your presentation, practice it. Plan what you'll do if something goes wrong.

3 Present

Introduce It

- State the title of your report; make it catchy.

- Grab the audience's attention with an interesting quote or story or a surprising statistic.

- State your main idea early and clearly.

- Let your audience know what they can expect to learn from your presentation.

Give Background Information

- Explain any important terms, history, or people that might be unfamiliar to your audience.

- Cover the basic information your listeners need to understand your presentation, but don't stray from your topic.

State Your Ideas

- Make three or four key points about your main idea.

- Supply at least two supporting details for each of your key points.

- Anticipate questions or objections and answer them before they're asked.

- Don't bore your audience with too many statistics. A few well-chosen, astounding facts will be more effective and memorable than ten forgettable ones.

- Use graphic aids to highlight information.

Wrap It Up in Your Conclusion

- Summarize by restating your main idea and key points.

- Finish on a positive note. If appropriate, you can suggest an action audience members can take.

- Leave your listeners with something to think about.

The "Tell 'Em" Plan

Good speakers help their audience listen and remember by introducing what they're going to say, saying it, and then reviewing it. This is sometimes called the "Tell 'Em" plan. Read the steps to see why.

◆ "Tell 'em what you're going to tell 'em" in your introduction.

◆ "Tell 'em" the main ideas and supporting details in the body of your speech.

◆ "Tell 'em what you told 'em" in your conclusion.

Speech-Making Tips

◆ Memorize your first and last sentences, but no more. If you try to memorize your whole speech and you forget one line or word, you won't have anything to fall back on. It's better to practice and use notes.

◆ Stand straight in a natural position. Don't sway.

◆ Use a podium or a pointer if you don't know what to do with your hands.

◆ If you feel nervous, take deep breaths to relax.

◆ Speak slowly and clearly. Speak loudly enough to be heard at the back of the room.

◆ Look at your audience. Make eye contact with people who look interested.

◆ Smile. Show enthusiasm. Look and sound interested in your topic.

Where Are You Going?

Summarize what you learned in this lesson. _____
_____
_____
_____

Now use your summary to write a *Take Charge!* goal that will help you become a better student.
_____
_____
_____

LESSON 27

Using Graphic Aids

Gem Name	Mineral	Usual Colors
Amethyst	quartz	purple
Diamond	carbon	bluish white
Emerald	beryl	green
Opal	opal	red, green, blue
Ruby	corundum	red
Sapphire	corundum	blue

Do you think it would be easier to learn this information by listening to it or by seeing it on a chart?

A Gem of an Idea

If you had heard the facts about gems in a speech instead of reading them in a chart, you might have found the information very confusing. The chart makes the information clearer and easier to understand. That's the purpose of all graphic aids—to help you understand and communicate information better.

As you prepare for a presentation, think about its contents. Which of your ideas could you show graphically? Then create and use photographs, charts, graphs, diagrams, or maps to enhance your presentation.

Where Do You Stand?

How familiar are you with the purposes of different types of graphic aids? Match each graphic aid in the first column with its purpose in the second column. Write the matching letter in the blank.

1. ____ Photograph

2. ____ Diagram

3. ____ Chart or table

4. ____ Map

5. ____ Graph

a. To show the parts or workings of something, usually with labels

b. To compare changes over time of two or more sets of information

c. To present a set of facts in an organized way, often in labeled columns

d. To help listeners visualize a setting, people, or other details mentioned in a speech

e. To show where things such as political boundaries, roads, or natural resources are located

Rate Yourself

How accurately did you identify the purposes of different types of graphic aids? Congratulations if you matched all five!

Is One Picture Worth a Thousand Words?

Sometimes a diagram can convey information better than words alone. Study the diagram below. Then ask a partner to draw a similar diagram by following your verbal instructions. Tell your partner not to look at this page until he or she is finished. Talk your partner through the drawing and try to help him or her "see" your description well enough to draw it. When the diagram is finished, discuss the number of words it took to describe a simple picture.

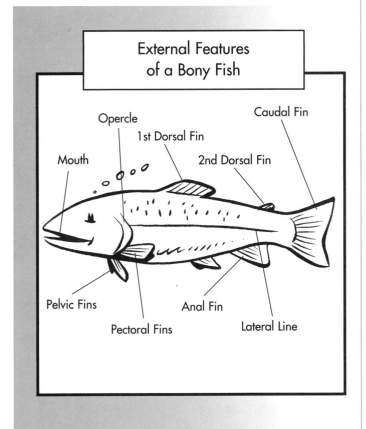

External Features
of a Bony Fish

Opercle
1st Dorsal Fin
Caudal Fin
Mouth
2nd Dorsal Fin
Pelvic Fins
Anal Fin
Pectoral Fins
Lateral Line

Choose the Most Effective Graphic Aid

Look for examples of graphic aids in your social studies textbook, magazines, or newspapers. Find at least one example of each of the following graphic aids:

- [ ] bar graph
- [ ] line graph
- [ ] circle graph or pie chart
- [ ] chart or table
- [ ] map

In a small group, analyze and compare the graphic aids. Discuss how effective they are in communicating information. Talk about why one type of graphic aid accompanies a certain type of article. For example, when is a map useful? When is a bar graph more appropriate than a circle graph? What type of information does a chart or table convey best? Write your conclusions in the chart below.

Graphic Aid:	Most Useful for:
bar graph	
line graph	
circle graph or pie chart	
chart or table	
map	

Seven Useful Graphic Aids

1 Diagrams

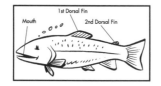

- Show the parts of something or how something works
- Useful for explaining detailed information
- Usually have labels that name the parts

2 Photographs

- Help your audience visualize a setting, people, or other things that may be unfamiliar to your listeners
- Often shown as part of the introduction. For example, for a speech about the Blue-Footed Booby, you might display a large photograph of the bird so the audience can visualize it

3 Maps

- Can be used to record and present many kinds of location information, such as geophysical features, political boundaries, roads, population distribution, weather, time zones, or natural resources
- Usually have a *legend*, or key, which identifies the map's symbols
- Often have a compass rose and a distance scale

4 Charts and Tables

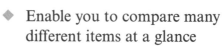

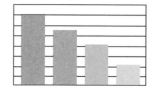

- Help organize statistics
- Enable you to compare many different items at a glance
- Usually organized in labeled columns and rows

5 Bar Graphs

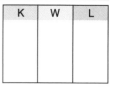

- Compare two or more sets of information
- Show how sets of facts are related
- Can be shown with vertical or horizontal bars, with each bar representing a measurement

6 Line Graphs

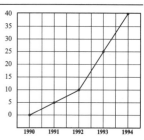

- Have points plotted on a scale and then joined by a line
- Often show a *trend*, which is the degree of change over a period of time
- Show an increase with an upward line
- Show a decrease with a downward line
- Show no change with a line that stays level

7 Circle Graphs

- Show how one part is related to the whole and to the other parts, with a circle representing 100%, or a whole amount
- Are divided into wedge-shaped slices, each representing a percentage of the whole
- Are often used to show how money is spent or to compare the relative sizes of populations or places

Helpful Hints for Graphic Aids

◆ Be sure to write the source of information on all your graphic aids.

◆ Give a descriptive title to every graphic aid you use.

◆ If necessary, include a legend explaining the features of a graph or map.

◆ Make your visuals as large as possible so people in the back of your audience can see them.

◆ Be neat. A carefully prepared graphic aid is impressive and will enhance your presentation. A sloppy one is difficult for the audience to understand and detracts from your presentation.

Take Note!

When preparing your graphic aids, write what you need to say about each one on an index card. If possible, tape the card on the back of the chart or poster so you can see it while the audience looks at the other side.

Wise Words

You're probably familiar with the Chinese proverb, "One picture is worth a thousand words." List reasons why a picture or other graphic aid can be "worth a thousand words" when you give a presentation.

_____

_____

_____

_____

_____

_____

_____

_____

_____

_____

Where Are You Going?

Summarize what you learned in this lesson. _____

_____

_____

_____

Now use your summary to write a *Take Charge!* goal that will help you become a better student.

_____

_____

_____

Personal Assessment Page

Congratulations! You've finished your *Take Charge!* book. You've completed the lessons and set goals to help you improve your study skills. By now, you've probably been able to make some changes and improvements in your study habits. Hopefully, you've seen some positive results!

This page is designed to help you and your teacher assess your progress. Here's how it works:

1. At the end of every lesson, you summarized what you learned and wrote a *Take Charge!* goal. Reread each of your summaries and goals.

2. Listed below are the titles of each unit of this book and a scale for assessing your progress. Think about the goals you set and the progress you have made. Then, assess yourself. Use the scale to record your progress.

3. Next, it's your teacher's turn. Your teacher will assess your progress using the same scale and his or her observations about your work.

When both assessments are complete, you and your teacher can compare and discuss the results. Together, you may come up with some ideas to improve your study skills even more. Like the title of this book says, *You Can Take Charge!*

Assessment Scale

1 = I do well in this area.
2 = I've made some changes and shown improvement.
3 = I've made some progress, but I still have a long way to go.
4 = I haven't worked on this. I'd better get started!

	My Assessment	My Teacher's Assessment
Managing Time, Materials, and Space		
Managing Yourself		
Working With Others		
Studying for Tests		
Developing Test-Taking Skills		
Participating in Class		
Working With Textbooks and References		
Preparing Speeches, Reports, and Projects		